THE
CHICAGO
CHEF'S TABLE

THE CHICAGO CHEF'S TABLE

EXTRAORDINARY RECIPES FROM THE WINDY CITY

2ND EDITION

AMELIA LEVIN

Globe
Pequot

Essex, Connecticut

Globe Pequot

An imprint of Globe Pequot, the trade division of
The Rowman & Littlefield Publishing Group, Inc.
4501 Forbes Blvd., Ste. 200
Lanham, MD 20706
www.rowman.com

Distributed by NATIONAL BOOK NETWORK

British Library Cataloguing in Publication Information Available

Library of Congress Cataloging-in-Publication Data

Names: Levin, Amelia, author.
Title: The Chicago chef's table : extraordinary recipes from the windy city /
Amelia Levin.
Description: Second edition. | Essex, Connecticut : Globe Pequot, 2023. |
"First edition published 2012".
Identifiers: LCCN 2022028411 (print) | LCCN 2022028412 (ebook) | ISBN
9781493044382 (cloth) | ISBN 9781493044399 (epub)
Subjects: LCSH: Cooking—Illinois—Chicago. | Restaurants—Illinois—
Chicago | LCGFT: Cookbooks.
Classification: LCC TX715 .L658 2023 (print) | LCC TX715 (ebook) | DDC
641.59773/11—dc23/eng/20220803
LC record available at https://lccn.loc.gov/2022028411
LC ebook record available at https://lccn.loc.gov/2022028412

♾️™ The paper used in this publication meets the minimum requirements
of American National Standard for Information Sciences—Permanence of
Paper for Printed Library Materials, ANSI/NISO Z39.48-1992.

To my husband, Harvey Henao, my rock and No. 1 taste tester, and children, Jonah and Liliana (taste testers-in-training).

CONTENTS

Acknowledgments | x

Introduction | xi

Starters and Salads | 1

Vie (Western Springs) and Gaijin | 2
Harvest Salad with Quick-Pickled Summer Beans
Okonomiyaki (Savory Japanese Pancake)

Galit | 5
Homemade Labneh (and Whey Brine)

North Pond | 7
Brazilian Cheese Bites

Takito Kitchen, Bar Takito, Takito Street | 10
Stuffed Colombian Arepas with Berkshire Pork Belly, Plantain, Black Beans, Avacado Puree, and Jicama

Roanoke | 12
Baby Beet and Farro Salad with Avocado, Tarragon, and Goat's Milk Feta

Monteverde | 14
Stuffed Focaccia with Mozzarella, Taggiasca, Olives, and Basil

Aba, Ēma | 16
Muhammara

mfk. | 18
Smoked Trout Salad

Le Sud | 21
Croquettes with Dijonnaise Dipping Sauce

Pasta and Noodles | 25

Piccolo Sogno | 26
Ravioli Quattro Formaggi (Four Cheese Ravioli)

Formento's, Nonna's, The Bristol | 28
Duck Egg Carbonara

Fisk & Co. | 30
Crab and Lobster Spaghetti

Daisies | 32
Agnolotti with Roasted Beets and Pickled Dill

Saranello's, Di Pescara | 35
Spinach and Ricotta Gnocchi
Tomato and Summer Squash Gratin

La Luna Chicago, Tree House | 40
Rigatoni with Crispy Prosciutto and Vodka Sauce

Fish | 43

Proxi | 44
Wild Striped Bass with Sweet Corn Chowder and Littleneck Clams

GT Fish & Oyster | 46
GT's Clam Chowder

Girl & the Goat, Little Goat, Duck Duck Goat, Cabra Cevicheria | 48
Mussels with Mighty Goat
    Sausage, Cilantro Butter, and
    Bagna Cauda Aioli

Lula Café, Marisol | 51
Milk-Poached Cod with White
    Asparagus and Charred
    Piquillo Peppers
Wisconsin Trout Soup with
    Potato-Infused Cream and
    Bacon

The Dearborn | 54
Grilled Swordfish Steak with Fava
    Bean Smash, Grilled Ramp
    Vinaigrette, Dates, Frisée and
    Hearts of Palm Salad

Osteria Langhe | 56
Risotto Certosino
Cipolla Arrosto

The Graceful Ordinary | 60
Steamed Mussels with Lobster
    Butter Sauce

LeTour | 62
Butter Basted Monkfish with
    Kohlrabi, Barley and Green
    Apple

Jeong | 64
Salmon Tartare with Doenjang
    and Yuzu Crème Fraîche

Mi Tocaya Antojeria | 66
Lobster Esquites

The Signature Room at the 95th | 68
Shrimp Dejonghe

Beef, Lamb and More | 71

Prairie Grass Café | 73
Grass-Fed Beef Brisket with Pan-
    Roasted Parsnips

Brindille, Kostali | 75
Walnut Crusted Veal Rib Eye with
    Gratin of Cauliflower, Pink
    Peppercorns, Confit Garlic,
    and Sage

Hopleaf | 78
Montreal-Style Smoked Brisket
    Sandwich

The Publican | 80
The Publican's Veal Sweetbreads

Beatnik and Porto | 82
Curried Meatballs with Avocado
    Hummus

Chez Moi | 84
Braised Lamb Shank
    Mediterranean

El Che Steakhouse & Bar | 86
Beef Tenderloin with Chimichurri

Pork | 89

avec/avec River North | 90
Chorizo-Stuffed Bacon-Wrapped
    Dates

The Purple Pig | 92
Milk-Braised Pork Shoulder and
    Creamy Mashed Potatoes

Big Star | 94
Tacos Al Pastor (Spit-Roasted
    Pork Tacos)

Swift & Sons | 96
Bacon-Wrapped Pork Loin
    Tonnato

Urban Belly | 98
Kimchi Stew with Braised Pork
Belly

Arun's | 100
Hung Lay Curry (turmeric-
marinated pork curry)

Café Ba-Ba-Reeba! | 102
Paella Mixta

Funkenhausen | 104
Pork Chops with Bourbon Sauce,
Carrot Puree and Spicy
Pepper Jelly

Rose Mary | 107
Pork Pampanella Ribs

**The Gage, Acanto, Beacon
Tavern | 109**
Scotch Eggs with Salad and
Mustard Vinaigrette

Poultry | 113

**Frontera Grill/
Topolobampo/XOCO | 114**
Carnitas de Pato (Chunks of
Duck Meat) with Crunchy
Tomatillo-Avocado Salsa

Le Colonial | 117
Ga Xao Xa Ot (Spicy Lemongrass
Chicken)

Summer House | 119
Santa Monica's Whole Roasted
Chicken

HBFC | 121
Buffalo Mac n' Cheese with
Chicken Crunchies
Honey Buffalo Pimento Mac n'
Cheese

**Superkhana
International | 124**
Butter Chicken Naan Calzone

Dessert | 129

Mindy's Bakery | 130
Grilled Marinated Doughnut
Peaches with Lemon Sabayon
and Poached Michigan
Blueberries

Robert Et Fils | 133
French Apple Cake

Dear Margaret | 135
Butter Tarts

Smyth and the Loyalist | 137
Chocolate Blackout Cake

Beatrix | 139
Gluten Free Tall, Dark and
Handsome Chocolate Cake

Photo Credits | 141

Index | 142

About the Author | 146

ACKNOWLEDGMENTS

"I love Chicago." In all my travels around the country and the world, I have yet to hear one person say something bad about this city. In fact, more often than not they've used those three simple words to describe it, as if the classic I-heart-NYC T-shirt had been made for us.

Chicago has a reputation for being a true Midwestern city—friendly folks, harsh winters, humid summers, and of course, good hearty food. In the last decade, though, our "Second City" has blossomed beyond the intrigue of the Mag Mile, endless skyscrapers and pretty coastline of salt-free water: Many now look at Chicago as a culinary mecca, rich with world-class restaurants and award-winning chefs that care just as strongly as they cook.

For that I deeply thank the talented chefs and restaurateurs for graciously and generously contributing tested recipes for this book, and for graciously and generously feeding this city and its visitors. I also thank them for shaping Midwestern fare into what it is now—farmer's market and seasonally-driven, creative, soulful, even whimsical—and for serving as culinary leaders in this country's quest to define and refine modern American cuisine.

I also thank my editor Amy Lyons and the team at Globe Pequot Press who worked with me on this second edition. Special thanks to Jenni Ferrari-Adler, my agent at Brickhouse Literary Agents, for believing in my ideas and helping them come to fruition.

INTRODUCTION

In the years since the first *Chicago Chef's Table* came out, the Windy City's culinary scene has seen many changes.

Restaurants have closed. Countless more have opened. Some concepts were re-concepted. The legendary stayed legendary. Buildings came down; others went up. The economy boomed. Then there was a global pandemic. The economy retracted. Then, it reacted. Though many restaurants closed during this time, still more opened or at least managed to remain open—even during such a tough time for the industry.

One thing has not changed. The vast majority of the Chicago chefs featured in the first book and others who came onto the scene afterward are All. Still. Here.

Sure, dining destination cities like New York, San Francisco and Los Angeles, and plenty of "mid-tier" markets like Austin, Denver and San Diego—with their warmer weather or lower rents—have beckoned these chefs. Regardless, so many have chosen to stay.

Sure, they may not be at the same restaurant or even at the same level that they were 10 years ago. But nonetheless, they're here, somewhere, cooking for us all. And we have been happily eating up all they have offered for the past decade.

This unwavering devotion and loyalty to a city that's often made fun of for its harsh winters and "casserole pizza" is still home—the only home—for so many Chicago chefs. It defines their character, their cooking style and their commitments, the latter of which have gone mostly to the communities they serve but also to the many growers, ranchers, fisheries, artisan food makers and other ingredient providers from the region.

That said, what else hasn't changed is this "farm-to-table" concept that was still a budding concept a decade ago. Now, it's just assumed that when you dine out at some of the best restaurants in Chicago, you'll be eating the best of the Midwest (or at least a sustainable product from elsewhere).

Ten years ago, diners may not have cared that much about taking pictures of their food with a phone, because most of our phones weren't good enough to do so. Now, chefs specifically prepare for the "carry over cooking" that happens when a perfectly plated dish begets a 5-minute, Instagram-worthy photo or Tik Tok video session.

In this new *Chicago Chef's Table*, you'll see some of the coveted recipes from the first book but with newer stories about where that chef has ended up today. Others added since then will tell stories about a handful of chefs who trained under those veterans but who have branched off on their own. We're on the third or fourth generation of Chicago chefs since the 1980s. And we've only just begun.

Some of the recipes in this book are replicas of dishes you once got or might get at the chef's restaurant. However, most are simply cherished dishes from chefs that speak to their cooking personalities. It's almost like you invited that person into your home to cook for you and your friends and family.

Some recipes in this new collection are simpler, with fewer steps but all the same deliciousness. Others require a little more care and precision—challenging even the best home cooks. Even non-cooks might find delight in just reading about some of Chicago's best and brightest.

There are regrettably many chefs we couldn't reach for this book, or who declined to participate for various reasons. (Some are coming out with their own cookbooks and need to hang on to every recipe they can!)

Still, we hope that by reading and cooking out of this book you'll see a nice snapshot of our food culture here in Chicago. Who knows, in another 10 (or 5 or 20) years it might and likely will look completely different. And that's a good thing.

One thing that won't change—of this we can be certain—the die-hard chefs of Chicago will still be the die-hard chefs of Chicago.

STARTERS AND SALADS

Two decades ago, the first grouping of dishes on a menu were simply called "appetizers." A decade ago, we called them "small plates." Now, you might see them listed on the menu as "snacks," "shared" or "to share." Push comes to shove, there are no rules when it comes to "starters" and salads—and the same goes for the recipes that follow. You want to make Chef Paul Virant's recipe for Okonomiyaki and eat it all by yourself? Go right ahead! In the mood to make a bigger batch of Chef Tim Vidrio's cheese bites for dinner guests coming over? That's the point! With these chef recipes at your fingertips, now you can create your own tasting menu, at home.

VIE anD GaIJIN

4471 Lawn Avenue, Western Springs
(708) 246-2082
Vierestaurant.com

950 W Lake Street, Chicago
(312) 265-1348
Gaijinchicago.com

After training at Chef Paul Kahan's legendary Blackbird, Chef Paul Virant moved with his wife, Jennifer, to Western Springs about 25 minutes outside of downtown Chicago, seeking to open his own spot. The result was Vie, which opened in 2004 and more than 15 years later is still a mainstay in the neighborhood. There, he focuses on classic, "farm-to-table" food with many pickled staples from his own garden, something Virant later became known for and even wrote a cookbook about. After a short time oversee-ing Perennial Virant at the Lincoln Hotel directly across the street from Lincoln Park, Virant turned his attention back toward Vie, growing his following even further.

During this time, ideas about a second restaurant—and a departure from his American cuisine—began to brew. "My wife studied Japanese in college at Duke and lived not far from Osaka," he says. "When we were dating, she introduced me to a classic Okonomiyaki, and at some point, I attempted to make it at home." After a trip to Tokyo and Osaka, the deal was sealed. Virant had to do a concept revolving around the addictive, Japanese savory pancake made with cabbage and grated yam that's topped with an alternating drizzle of tangy sauce and Kewpie mayo, along with tempura flakes that wave tenderly in the air when transported to the table. He opened Gaijin, which means "outsider," as in a self-described word for himself, in 2019.

HARVEST SALAD WITH QUICK-PICKLED SUMMER BEANS

(SERVES 4)

For the quick-pickled summer beans:

1 pound summer beans (green beans and/or yellow wax beans), trimmed and washed

1 cup water

2 cups champagne vinegar

2 teaspoons sugar

1 teaspoon kosher salt

1 teaspoon crushed red pepper flakes

3 sprigs fresh dill

1 teaspoon dill seed

1 teaspoon black peppercorns

For the salad:

2 tablespoons grapeseed oil

1 cup trimmed, cored, and quartered brussels sprouts

2 cups pickled beans

1 medium hakuri turnip (or salad turnip), trimmed and thinly sliced

1 medium Honey Crisp apple, sliced

1 small red onion, thinly sliced

1 cup flat-leaf parsley leaves

¼ cup extra-virgin olive oil

Kosher salt and pepper, to taste

Rustic croutons and freshly grated Pecorino Romano cheese (optional garnish)

To prepare the beans: Blanch the beans in a large pot of boiling salted water for 1 minute; drain. Place beans in a container large enough to hold brine. Combine remaining 8 ingredients in a saucepan and bring to a boil. Pour brine over beans. The liquid should cover the beans (to help cover, place a large resealable plastic bag filled with water on top). Cool completely and refrigerate. Beans are ready immediately but could be prepared up to a week ahead.

Strain the beans, reserving ¼ cup of the pickled bean liquid. Bring this liquid to a boil in a small saucepan and reduce by half. Set aside.

To prepare the salad: Heat the grapeseed oil over medium-high heat in a large sauté pan. Add brussels sprouts and cook until caramelized and tender, about 5 minutes. Transfer to a medium bowl and cool.

Add the beans, turnip, apple, onion, and parsley to the brussels sprouts. Whisk together olive oil, reduced bean liquid, salt, and pepper. Add dressing to bowl, toss to coat. Divide salad among four plates. Garnish with croutons and cheese, if desired.

OKONOMIYAKI (SAVORY JAPANESE PANCAKE)
(SERVES 2)

For the pancakes:

1 cup dashi

½ cup finely grated yam (note: best with traditional nagaimo found at Asian groceries)

2 eggs

⅔ cup all-purpose flour

1 teaspoon baking powder

3½ cups Napa cabbage, chopped

2 or 3 scallions, thinly sliced (about 1 cup)

1 tablespoon minced ginger or pickled ginger

Sea or kosher salt, to taste

½ cup tempura flakes (tenkatsu)

Vegetable oil

3 slices bacon, cut in half

For the garnish:

Mayonnaise or Japanese Kewpie mayonnaise

Okonomiyaki sauce (bottled, purchased online or homemade, recipe below*)

Aonori (dried green seaweed), optional

Katsuobushi (bonito flakes)

For the okonomiyaki sauce:

4 tablespoons ketchup

3½ tablespoons Worcestershire sauce

2 tablespoons oyster sauce

1½ tablespoons sugar, honey, or pure maple syrup

Preheat griddle, large skillet or cast-iron pan to medium-high heat.

To prepare the pancakes: In a large mixing bowl, combine dashi, yam and eggs; whisk well to combine. Add flour and baking powder; mix well. Add cabbage, scallions and pickled ginger; mix well. Season with salt.

Fold in tempura flakes.

Brush vegetable oil on griddle or pan and divide batter into 2 portions on the griddle. Spread out with a spatula to form an even circle, place 3 halves of bacon on each; cover each with a lid. Cook for 4 minutes.

Uncover and flip pancakes. Cook another 4 minutes until cooked through. Brush okonomiyaki sauce on pancakes and add a zig-zag drizzle of mayonnaise or Kewpie. Sprinkle aonori and/or bonito flakes over all and serve.

*To prepare the okonomiyaki sauce: Combine all ingredients in a medium bowl and whisk well. Refrigerate for up to 2 weeks.

GALIT

2429 N Lincoln Avenue
(773) 360-8755
Galitrestaurant.com

Chef Zachary Engel trained with famed New Orleans chef Alon Shaya, helping lead the team to take home the 2016 James Beard Award for Best New Restaurant in 2016 and earning him the James Beard Rising Star Chef of the Year Award in 2017 before moving to Chicago to open his first restaurant, Galit, with business partner Andrés Clavero. Engel's career also includes time spent in the kitchens of Zahav in Philadelphia, Catit in Tel Aviv and the Michelin-starred Madrona Manor in Sonoma County. Those experiences, combined with growing up in a Jewish household as the son of a rabbi are the grounding elements of his modern Middle Eastern cooking at the acclaimed Galit. Here, Engel offers a recipe for homemade labneh, which is a farmer's cheese made from straining a seasoned yogurt. "We use whole milk, full fat yogurt so the labneh is full bodied and rich," he says. "If you don't refrigerate the yogurt as it drains, it gets a little funky and fermented, which tastes even better. The 'whey brine' is the water that drains off the yogurt. It's like using a buttermilk brine, which tenderizes the meat and keeps it moist even if you overcook it a little bit. It's our go-to for seasoning chicken at Galit." At Galit, labneh is served as part of a mezze platter with hummus and other dips, along with homemade pita bread and raw and pickled vegetables. It makes for the perfect party dish or shared snack.

HOMEMADE LABNEH (AND WHEY BRINE)

(MAKES 2 CUPS)

For the labneh:

4 cups whole milk yogurt

3 tablespoons salt

1 piece of cheesecloth

For the whey brine:

1 tablespoon salt

1 tablespoon white granulated sugar

4 chicken thighs, boneless, skin-on

To prepare the labneh: Place the yogurt in a large mixing bowl. Add the salt and mix in with a whisk until thoroughly combined.

Place a large colander inside of a large bowl and line the colander with 5 to 7 layers of cheesecloth. Pour the yogurt-salt mixture into the colander and then cover with plastic wrap. Refrigerate for at least 24 hours to drain.

The next day, pull the labneh out of the cheesecloth and keep refrigerated. It should be thick like cream cheese. The texture will tighten even more as it gets colder in the refrigerator. Serve labneh slightly chilled or at room temperature with pita bread and crudité for dipping.

To prepare the whey brine: Reserve the "whey" that has drained from the yogurt. Add the remaining tablespoon of salt and tablespoon of sugar to the brine and whisk until dissolved. Place the chicken thighs in a medium bowl or plastic bag and cover with the seasoned yogurt whey. Marinate for at least 4 hours then drain off the brain and pat the chicken thighs dry with a paper towel before baking or grilling and serving with more labneh for a sauce.

NORTH POND

2610 N Cannon Drive
(773) 477-5845
Northpondrestaurant.com

Once a warming house for ice-skaters on the pond at the north end of Lincoln Park, the quaint stone building that is North Pond Restaurant has been providing a quiet refuge amid the bustling urban jungle for more two decades. The brainchild of legendary Chicago chef Bruce Sherman, North Pond has seen the likes of regulars and celebratory guests alike, known as one of the first fine-dining American restaurants in the city and country. Though now retired, Sherman is known for being a pioneer in the farm-to-table movement, well before it became a trend or even the norm. He was one of the founding members of Green City Market, Chicago's longstanding farmer's market in the heart of Lincoln Park just a short jaunt from the restaurant. In addition to showcasing the best of the Midwest, North Pond has served as the training ground for many successful chefs in the city. These Brazilian Cheese Bites, developed by the North Pond culinary team, first made their debut on a new bar snacks menu but have stood the test of time.

BRAZILIAN CHEESE BITES

(MAKES ABOUT 24 BITES)

½ cup plus 1 tablespoon unsalted butter or grapeseed oil

2½ cups apple cider

1 teaspoon kosher salt

3 cups tapioca flour or tapioca starch

6 large eggs

3 cups grated Parmesan or other aged hard cheese

1 teaspoon grated nutmeg

¼ teaspoon cayenne

Zest from 2 lemons

Chopped chives or parsley (optional)

Soft cheese (such as brie or Greyson cheese) or seasonal jam, for the filling

Confectioner's sugar (optional)

In a medium saucepot, combine the butter, cider and salt and bring to a simmer, stirring to combine. Sprinkle in the tapioca starch and gently cook to hydrate the starch, mixing well first with a whisk and then with a heat resistant spatula until a thick paste forms. Continue to cook, stirring constantly to ensure the bottom of the pot does not burn, until thickened and flour taste is gone, about two minutes.

Remove from the heat and pour the mixture into the bowl of an eclectic stand mixer fitted with the paddle attachment. Mix on low to release excess heat/steam, about 1 minute. Add eggs, one at a time, while mixing on low until incorporated completely.

Add the cheese, nutmeg, cayenne, lemon zest and herbs (if using). Mix on low until a soft dough forms. Remove from the bowl, wrap in plastic wrap and refrigerate for two hours.

Preheat the oven to 400°F.

Spray two 12-cup or one 24-cup (2-inch by 1.25-inch deep) muffin tins with cooking spray. Fill each cup with 2 tablespoons of dough (just under halfway). Bake for 20 minutes, rotating the pan at the 10-minute mark to ensure even baking. After 20 minutes, reduce the oven temperature to 325°F and continue to bake to crisp up and dry out the center of the pastry, up to an additional 20 minutes. Cool on a wire rack.

Once cooled, the pastry will be hollow in the center. Fill a pastry bag or plastic bag fitted with a small piping tip with softened cheese or seasonal jam. Fill each cheese bite with about a teaspoon or so of the filling. If desired, sprinkle with powdered sugar and serve warm.

CHICAGO PIZZA

Ultra-thick, stringy cheese, sweet tomato sauce, butter crust, the occasional fennel-spiked sausage. Chicago's known for many things—the wind, shopping along Mag Mile, the skyscrapers, snowy winters, and hot humid summers at the beach. It's also a rich food-lover's dream, from the char-grilled burgers and ballpark dogs, to stuffed burritos, Italian beef sandwiches, caramel popcorn, and of course, deep dish pizza.

Deep dish pizza, a stringent departure from the thinner, chewier crust pizza found in New York, was born at Pizzeria Uno on Ohio Street in the 1940s after owner Ric Riccardo looked for something heartier to serve Chicagoans than the traditional thin-crust version. But Riccardo's not credited with the pie's actual invention—historians still debate over whether it was Riccardo, who died in the 1950s, his business partner Ike Sewell, or Rudy Malnati, then the manager who later went on to open Pizzeria Due across the street. That later led to another famous deep dish pizza chain in the Malnati family: Lou Malnati's, and then there's also Pizano's from the same family. Now, deep dish joints in Chicago run the gamut, from Gino's to Giordano's, Pequod's to Renaldi's, Aurelio's to Edwardo's, and the list goes on.

Described as a cheese casserole in a cast-iron pan, Uno's and Malnati's especially have been able to achieve that crackly, slightly caramelized crunch from the buttery, shortbread crust thanks to its seasoned pans (which don't see much soap and water) and double-stacked, super-hot ovens. Sausage is the most popular, but pepperoni, spinach, and plain old cheese are old standbys. Tableside, most Chicagoans sprinkle their slice (or slices) with oregano, Parmesan cheese and red pepper flakes.

Many restaurateurs and chefs have chosen to escape the heaviness of deep dish and produce pizzas that go back to their Italian roots. The pies have doughier, chewier crusts commonly found in Rome and Naples that are then charred in wood-burning or even coal-fired ovens.

Some Chicago restaurateurs have gone off in different directions, replicating the pizzas from their hometowns, be it New Haven-style, with its white sauce and clams, or Detroit-style, with its rectangular shape and caramelized edges. And then there is the "other" classic, Chicago pizza popularized by many old school haunts: Tavern-style, a thinner, cracker crust pie that's sliced into squares (no folding allowed). Regardless of which style you prefer, or the mood you're in, when it comes to pizza, Chicago has it all.

Takito Kitchen, Bar Takito, Takito Street

2013 W Division Street
(773) 687-9620
Takitokitchen.com

201 N Morgan Street
(312) 888-9485
Bartakito.com

2423 N Lincoln Avenue
(773) 697-3132
Takitostreet.com

It was the scent of his grandmother's sourdough bread, enjoying a meal cooked by a friend's French mother and eating a whole head of roasted garlic for the first time at a restaurant when he was young that paved Chef David Dworshak's passion for cooking and food. After working at local restaurants as a teenager, Dworshak moved to Chicago to earn an associate's degree from Le Cordon Bleu Cooking & Hospitality Institute in 2001 after studying biology and French at the University of South Alabama. During culinary school, Dworshak worked under Chef Allen Stern-weller at Harvest on Huron, later becoming an assistant to Chef Mark Mendez (Carnivale, Vera). They bonded immediately, and Dworshak counts Mendez as a mentor. It was at Carnivale, restaurateur Jerry Kleiner's Central and South American restaurant, while serving as executive chef, that he developed this recipe for Colombian arepas. In 2013, Dworshak left Carnivale to open Takito Kitchen in Wicker Park, where he created a Latin American concept focusing on unique tacos and small plates. The restaurant group now includes Bar Takito in the West Loop and Takito Street in Lincoln Park.

STUFFED COLOMBIAN AREPAS WITH BERKSHIRE PORK BELLY, PLANTAIN, BLACK BEANS, AVOCADO PUREE, AND JICAMA

(SERVES 6)

For the Berkshire pork belly:

1-2 ounces salt

1 tablespoon freshly ground black pepper

1-2 ounces brown sugar

1 teaspoon ground coriander

1 teaspoon cayenne pepper

1 teaspoon dried oregano

1 pound pork belly

For the arepas:

2 cups masarepa flour*

2 cups hot water

2 tablespoons lard or butter

Salt and pepper, to taste

For the avocado puree:

2 ripe avocadoes, peeled, pitted, and diced

2 tablespoons fresh lime juice

1 tablespoon sautéed minced garlic

1 tablespoon chopped cilantro

1 serrano chile, minced

Salt and pepper, to taste

For the stuffing:

1 cup fried sweet plantains (packaged or freshly made)

1 cup canned black beans, drained and rinsed

1 cup queso Cotija or Monterey Jack cheese, shredded, or crumbled queso fresco

1 clove minced garlic

1 fresh jicama, peeled and sliced into 1-inch-long pieces

Hot sauce

To prepare the Berkshire pork belly: In a small bowl, mix together all the dry ingredients for the pork belly and rub thoroughly over the meat. Wrap and refrigerate for at least 1-2 hours, up to three days.

Heat the oven to 425°F. Roast pork belly, fat side up, until browned, about 20 minutes. Reduce oven temperature to 300°F and continue to roast pork until fork tender, about 1 hour. Set aside.

To prepare the arepa: Combine all ingredients for the arepa in a large bowl and mix until well combined. Roll dough into 3–4-ounce balls and flatten to 1½-inch thickness. Thoroughly grease a large sauté pan or griddle and cook arepas over medium-high heat until browned, about 2-3 minutes per side.

To prepare the avocado puree: Combine all the ingredients in a food processor or blender and process until smooth, about 1 minute. Alternatively, mash the ingredients by hand with a potato masher. Set aside.

To prepare the stuffing: Mix the plantains, beans, cheese, and garlic in medium bowl until well combined. Set aside.

To serve: Split each arepa in half horizontally, leaving a hinge attached. Stuff with the browned pork belly, plantain mixture, jicama, hot sauce, and a dollop of avocado puree.

*Masarepa flour, a dried, precooked ground corn flour used for arepas, can be found in most South American specialty markets. Different from masa harina, used for making tortillas, masarepa may also be labeled *masa al instante* or *harina precocida* by such brands as Goya, Juana, and Harina.

ROANOKE

135 W Madison Street
(312) 361-3800
Theroanokerestaurant.com

A Midwestern native, Chef Greg Elliot graduated from culinary school at Kendall College and went on to work at various acclaimed restaurants in Chicago, including Ambira, Naha, Aubriot and One Sixtyblue. For a short time, he ventured out to Napa Valley to helm the kitchen at Brannan's Grill, returning to the Windy City in 2010. During that time, he served as executive chef at the former Lockwood restaurant in the historic Palmer House Hilton as well as at Current and Remington's. After joining Roanoke Hospitality in 2018 as executive chef, he quickly elevated the new restaurant's status as a culinary powerhouse and supporter of local food and farms with a strong cocktail menu and private event offerings.

BABY BEET AND FARRO SALAD WITH AVOCADO, TARRAGON, AND GOAT'S MILK FETA

(SERVES 4-6)

For the farro:

1 tablespoon extra-virgin olive oil

1 onion, diced

3 cups uncooked farro

Water or vegetable broth

Salt and pepper, to taste

For the beets:

1 pound trimmed baby beets

2 tablespoons extra-virgin olive oil

Salt and freshly ground black pepper

For the lemon vinaigrette and assembly:

½ cup fresh lemon juice

¼ cup sherry vinegar

1¼ cups plus 2 tablespoons extra-virgin olive oil, divided

Salt and freshly ground black pepper

2 shallots, sliced

3 tablespoons chopped fresh tarragon

Zest of 1 lemon

2 ripe avocados, in large dice

2 heads frisée, cleaned

1 cup crumbled goat's milk feta (preferably Redwood Hill Farms)

1 tablespoon honey

To prepare the farro: Heat the oil in a sauté pan over medium heat and cook onions until lightly browned, about 5 minutes. Stir in farro and enough water or broth just to cover. Bring to a light simmer. Cook slowly, stirring occasionally and adding more water each time the liquid reduces. Continue cooking 30-35 minutes or until farro is tender. Season with salt and pepper to taste and refrigerate until chilled.

To prepare the beets: Preheat oven to 400°F. Toss beets with the olive oil, salt, and pepper to taste. Roast on a sheet pan for 40-45 minutes or until cooked through. Allow the beets to cool and remove the skin with a paring knife or paper towel. Quarter beets and reserve for salad.

To prepare lemon vinaigrette: Whisk together the lemon juice and vinegar. Slowly pour in 1¼ cups olive oil, whisking constantly. Season with salt and pepper to taste. In a large bowl, toss farro with half of the shallots and tarragon, the lemon vinaigrette, and lemon zest. In another bowl, toss together the beets, avocados, and remaining shallots and tarragon.

To serve: Toss the frisée with 1 tablespoon olive oil, salt, and pepper to taste. Spoon the farro salad onto the bottom of a large platter and top with the beet mixture, frisée salad, and feta cheese. Drizzle honey and the remaining 1 tablespoon olive oil on and around the salad to finish.

MONTEVERDE

1020 W Madison Street
(312) 888-3041
Monteverdechicago.com

Sarah Grueneberg rose to the top ranks of Chicago's culinary scene while at the legendary Spiaggia. Originally from Houston, Grueneberg moved to Chicago in 2005 to join the team at Tony Mantuano's award-winning restaurant, first as a line cook and later rising the ranks to Chef di Cucina in 2008 and Executive Chef in 2010. During her tenure as head she earned the restaurant a coveted Michelin Star for three consecutive years. Grueneberg became more well-known nationally after making it to the finals of Bravo TV's ninth season of *Top Chef*, filmed in her home state of Texas. In 2015, she opened her own restaurant, Monteverde Restaurant & Pastificio in Chicago's West Loop, with business partner and long-time friend Meg Sahs. The restaurant has received acclaimed reviews from various outlets and helped Grueneberg earn the James Beard Foundation Award for "Best Chef: Great Lakes" in 2017.

Her restaurant was awarded "Restaurant of the Year" in 2018 at the Jean Banchet Awards. For her focaccia recipe, Grueneberg reaches for Taggiasca olives, which are small, reddish-brown olives grown in the Liguria region on the northwest coast of Italy that have a delicate, slightly fruity taste. If you can't find these olives, substitute Gaeta or other semi-ripe olives and omit the salt in the stuffing mixture.

STUFFED FOCACCIA WITH MOZZARELLA, TAGGIASCA, OLIVES, AND BASIL
(SERVES 12-15)

For the dough:

2 packets (¼-ounce each) active dry yeast

Pinch of sugar

2 cups warm water (110°F)

6 tablespoons extra-virgin olive oil, divided

5 cups all-purpose flour

2 teaspoons sea salt

2 tablespoons cornmeal

For the stuffing:

4 ounces fresh mozzarella cheese, thinly sliced

1 cup loosely packed basil leaves

½ cup (2 ounces) grated Parmigiano Reggiano cheese

1 cup pitted Taggiasca olives, divided

Sea salt and freshly ground black pepper, to taste

To prepare the dough: Combine yeast, sugar, and water in a small bowl and let sit until bubbly, about 5 minutes. Stir in 2 tablespoons of the olive oil.

Add the flour and salt to the bowl of an electric stand mixer fitted with a dough hook. Add the yeast mixture and mix on low speed until the dough pulls away from the sides of the bowl, about 3-5 minutes.

Transfer the dough to a lightly oiled bowl. Turn over to coat lightly. Cover with a clean towel and let rise in a warm place 1 hour or until doubled in size.

Place dough on a countertop lightly dusted with flour. Knead dough until a smooth ball forms, about 5 minutes. Divide dough into 2 equal balls; cover with a clean towel or plastic wrap and let rest 15 minutes.

Preheat oven to 300°F. Brush a 12 x 18-inch baking sheet with 2 tablespoons of the olive oil and sprinkle with cornmeal. Press one ball of dough evenly into the baking pan to form the bottom crust.

To assemble the stuffing: Layer mozzarella cheese, basil, Parmigiano Reggiano cheese, and ¾ cup of the olives over crust. Season with salt and pepper to taste.

Roll out remaining ball of dough to the same size as the pan. Place over filled dough. Brush 2 tablespoons olive oil over dough. Garnish with the remaining olives by pushing them a half inch down into the top layer of dough. Cover with foil; bake for 30 minutes. Uncover; continue to bake 15 minutes, or until crust is golden brown and toothpick inserted in center comes out clean. Drizzle lightly with additional oil. Allow bread to cool in pan 20 minutes before slicing to serve.

ABa, ĒMa

302 N Green Street, 3rd Floor
(773) 645-1400
Abarestaurants.com

74 W Illinois Street
(312) 527-5586
Emachicago.com

Chef CJ Jacobsen brought a little bit of the West Coast for the menu at Aba and Ēma, which both feature a light and bright, modern take on Middle Eastern cuisine. "I would call it Eastern Mediterranean food seen through the eyes of a chef from California," says Jacobsen, who was born in Orange County and, while on a college volleyball scholarship, traveled throughout Belgium, Israel, and the Netherlands, where he discovered food could be exciting and inspiring. Returning to Los Angeles, he enrolled at the Le Cordon Bleu-affiliated College of Culinary Arts in Pasadena, graduating in 2004 and taking his first job at Axe, a highly regarded restaurant with an ingredient-driven, California menu. After his first appearance on Bravo TV's *Top Chef* in 2007, Jacobsen worked as executive chef at The Yard, a gastropub in Santa Monica, California. The following year, Jacobsen participated in the James Beard Celebrity Chef Tour and in 2012, he staged at the world-renowned Copenhagen restaurant Noma, working closely with acclaimed Chef René Redzepi. It was there he honed his skills with and appreciation for every single ingredient—foraging for it, exploring it, and researching it.

In July 2013, he become the executive chef at Girasol restaurant in Studio City, California and a year later was brought in as the first chef-in-residence at Intro in Chicago, which earned three stars from the *Chicago Tribune*. Now, as part of the Lettuce Entertain You Enterprises family, Jacobsen continues to focus on light, Mediterranean-style cooking using healthful and unique spices and ingredients. His muhammara recipe, Jacobsen says, is a little less traditional and more of his own interpretation. "Muhammara is great for when you're having people over or are feeding a group," he says. "It has a really nice, slightly crunchy mouthfeel and the pomegranate adds a little sweetness and tang on top of the floral flavors." He recommends serving a big bowl of the chunky pepper-spice-walnut condiment like a dip, with fresh pita bread or pita chips, crudité, and/ or even tortillas.

MUHAMMARA
(MAKES ABOUT 3 CUPS)

1 clove garlic

Juice from 1 lemon

1 (16-ounce) jar roasted red bell peppers (drained)

1 cup whole walnuts, toasted

2 teaspoons ground Aleppo pepper

2 teaspoons ground isot chili (optional)

2 teaspoons cumin

¼ cup tomato paste

2 tablespoons pomegranate molasses

1 teaspoon soy sauce

¼ teaspoon freshly ground black pepper

Pinch salt, or to taste

Add garlic and lemon juice to the bowl of a food processor. Pulse until garlic is just chopped. Allow to sit for five minutes. This helps tone down the raw garlic taste.

Add the bell peppers, walnuts, Aleppo pepper, isot chili (if using) and cumin. Pulse until mixture is fully combined but still chunky.

Transfer mixture to a large bowl and fold in the remaining ingredients. Season with salt.

Cover and refrigerate until use or serve immediately at room temperature with pita bread and/or crudité.

MFK.

432 W Diversey Parkway
(773) 857-2540
Mfkrestaurant.com

At the young age of 23 years old, the on-the-job-trained, natural talent Chef Alisha Elenz was promoted to executive chef of the Michelin Bib Gourmand award-winning restaurant, mfk. Since then, she has earned the Jean Banchet Award for Rising Star Chef and was a finalist for the James Beard Rising Star Chef, among other accolades. A native of the Chicagoland area, Elenz started out working at her uncle's pizzeria with no intention of staying in the restaurant industry. But a love of cooking drew her back, and soon after moving downtown, she got the opportunity to stage at Maude's Liquor Bar, part of Brandon Sodikoff's Hogsalt Hospitality restaurant group. "That was a huge transition because it turned out that was the kind of food I wanted to focus on," says Elenz, referring to the fresh seafood and raw bar program the now-closed restaurant boasted. The on-the-job-trained chef with a natural talent who grew up learning to cook with her Italian family, went on to work in the kitchens at the Waldorf-Astoria restaurant. But she soon tired of hotel work and longed for a smaller, independent outpost where she could forge her own path.

When a friend working at the then 9-month-old mfk. alerted her to a part-time line cook job in 2015, she took it on full force. The hard work paid off; she was named executive chef just two years later. The promotions continued; when the restaurant group opened Bar Biscay, a more casual, bar-driven outpost in 2018, she took over the kitchen operations at that time, becoming a partner in the business owned by the husband-wife duo Scott Worsham and Sari Zernich Worsham. That second location, sadly, closed during the height of the coronavirus pandemic of 2020, but Elenz has remained steadfast with mfk. There, rather than just "throwing traditional Spanish food" at people, she uses it more as an influencer for her seafood-heavy program, incorporating many Midwestern, seasonal ingredients and flavors for a mashup menu that she changes regularly.

Her recipe for a smoked trout salad has been a top seller when featured on her menu. At mfk., she cures and smokes her own fish in house, starting with sourcing steelhead trout fillets, which are cured in a dry cure for roughly four hours. The trout fillets are then rubbed down with a sherry aioli and smoked with apple wood chips. The method for smoking your own trout is included here, but you can also purchase pre-smoked trout, a common ingredient found throughout the Midwest, from a reputable fishmonger.

SMOKED TROUT SALAD
(SERVES 2)

For the salad:

1 tablespoon freshly squeezed lemon juice

3 tablespoons extra-virgin olive oil

2 cups chopped frisée lettuce

2 radishes, sliced

1 cup haricot verts (French green beans), sliced on a diagonal into ¼-inch pieces

2 tablespoons chopped parsley

2 tablespoons chopped chives

4 to 6 ounces smoked trout

For the toast:

2 large, thick-cut pieces sourdough bread

2 tablespoons butter

½ cup slivered almonds

For the garlic relish (optional):

½ cup minced garlic

Pinch of lemon zest

2 tablespoons lemon juice

1 teaspoon salt

Pinch freshly ground black pepper

1 cup white vinegar

For the green goddess dressing:
(Makes about 3½ cups)

3 egg yolks

6 anchovies, packed in oil, drained

2 tablespoons lemon juice

2 tablespoons crème fraîche

2 tablespoons Dijon mustard

2 tablespoons sherry vinegar

1 teaspoon minced shallot

1 teaspoon minced or 2 cloves garlic

2 teaspoons chopped parsley and/or chives

1½ tablespoon chopped dill

2 teaspoons salt

Pinch of freshly ground black pepper

⅓ cup extra-virgin olive oil, plus more as needed

For the olive chimichurri:
(Makes about 1¾ cups)

½ cup marinated olives, drained (from a bottle or salad bar at grocery store)

¼ cup liquid from marinated olives

4 tablespoons minced shallots

1 teaspoon chopped parsley or chives

2 tablespoons sherry vinegar

4 tablespoons extra-virgin olive oil

To prepare the garlic relish: Add all of the ingredients except for the vinegar to a small bowl or jar. In a small skillet, bring the vinegar to a light boil. Pour the hot vinegar over the other ingredients in the bowl or jar. Cover and set aside to cool, then refrigerate to cool completely.

To prepare the green goddess dressing: Combine all the ingredients, except for the oil, in a food processor. Pulse until chunky. With the motor running, add the oil and pulse until just emulsified, adding more oil as needed. The dressing won't be too thick, but it should also not be a loose consistency. Alternatively, use a hand-held immersion blender to make the dressing. Set aside.

To prepare the olive chimichurri: Slice olives into quarters and place in a small bowl. Add the shallots and herbs and mix. Add the vinegar, reserved marinade from olives, and olive oil, mixing to combine. Set aside.

To prepare the toast: Heat butter in a skillet over medium heat. Add almonds and sourdough bread slices and let sit, flipping bread once, until bread and almonds are lighted toasted and browned, about 2 minutes per side. Remove from heat and set aside.

To prepare the salad: Place the olive oil and lemon juice in a large bowl. Whisk vigorously to combine. Add the frisée, radish, haricot verts, 2 tablespoons of the drained garlic relish (if using), parsley, chives and smoked trout. Toss to lightly coat.

To serve: Divide salad between plates. Serve with a slice of the bread and some of the toasted almonds. Top with a light drizzle of the green goddess dressing and about a heaping tablespoon or so of olive chimichurri on the side.

LE SUD

2301 W Roscoe Street
(773) 857-1985
Lesudchicago.com

You'll find Chef Michael Woodhall's recipe for croquettes on the menu at Le Sud, restauranteur Sandy Chen's first foray into Provençal French and Mediterranean food (her first restaurant, Koi Fine Asian Cuisine & Lounge, is located in downtown Evanston). Opened in 2018 in the heart of the residential-heavy Roscoe Village neighborhood on Chicago's North Side, Le Sud has become a local favorite, especially for al fresco dining. Woodhall, a native of Hinsdale, Illinois, began his culinary career in high school, cooking at neighborhood restaurants, he says to collect money for concert tickets. A ski and snowboard enthusiast, he graduated from Colorado Mountain College's Culinary Arts Program in 2004, remaining in Colorado to work as grill cook at Remington's at The Ritz-Carlton, followed by sous chef at Toscanini in Beaver Creek. In 2010, Woodhall returned to Chicago as chef de partie at Perennial Virant in Lincoln Park, and a year later, joined Hogsalt Hospitality to serve as chef de partie at Gilt Bar, followed by executive chef of Bavette's Bar & Boeuf. Woodhall joined the opening team at Le Sud in 2018, moving up the ranks from line cook to sous chef and then to executive chef. Woodhall focuses on intense flavors and recognizable Provençal dishes with a nod to the Mediterranean and its fresh seafood, good olive oil, garlic and seasonal vegetables.

CROQUETTES WITH DIJONNAISE DIPPING SAUCE
(MAKES 5 CROQUETTES)

For the batter:

1¼ cups water

½ cup plus 1 tablespoon butter

1 cup all-purpose flour

4.5 ounces gruyere cheese

8.75 ounces diced ham

2 tablespoons salt, plus more for serving

5 whole eggs

Canola, vegetable or other high-heat oil, for frying

For the Dijonnaise:

1 cup good-quality or homemade mayonnaise

1 teaspoon lemon juice

2 teaspoons garlic powder

1 tablespoon Dijon mustard

To prepare the Dijonnaise: Whisk together all the ingredients for the dipping sauce in a small bowl. Cover and refrigerate until serving.

To prepare the batter: Bring water and butter in a large saucepot to a boil. Add flour, stirring vigorously until a dough forms. Continue to cook until raw flour smell is cooked out, about 2 minutes.

Transfer batter to an electric stand mixer fitted with the paddle attachment. Mix on low for 2 minutes to release some heat. Add the cheese, ham and salt and mix for 2 minutes. Add eggs, 1 at a time while mixing on low, until fully incorporated.

Pour oil into a wide, deep saucepot or Dutch oven to cover the sides 3 inches up from the bottom. Heat oil to 350°F.

Working in 2 batches so as not to reduce oil temperature, using a metal spoon or ice cream scoop, scoop about 1 ounce (2 tablespoons) of batter in a ball shape and drop into the simmering oil. Fry until browned, flipping once, about 2 to 3 minutes.

Drain on a paper towel-lined large plate or sheet tray. Lightly season croquettes with salt before serving warm with the Dijonnaise on the side.

PASTA AND NOODLES

Chicago has a rich Italian heritage and that's reflected not only by Little Italy and the immigrants who wove the city's cultural fabric years ago but also by the chefs who have devoted their work to this particular cuisine, and still others who have found inspiration in Italian ingredients and dishes. In many ways, Italian food here, and nationwide, no longer represents an "ethnic" food. It's become a way of eating and a way of life.

Still, when we talk about pasta in relation to Chicago, other types of noodles must not go unnoticed. From the brothy, steaming bowls of ramen at Urbanbelly to the pho, pad Thai and udon noodle soup that abound everywhere in between, Chicago enjoys culinary influences from many Asian immigrants and neighborhood communities, including Japanese, Thai and Korean as well as Little Vietnam near Argyle Street and China Town farther South.

PICCOLO SOGNO

464 North Halsted Street, River West
(312) 421-0077
Piccolosognorestaurant.com

Tony Priolo has a lot of friends. It started during his 12-year tenure as executive chef of Coco Pazzo in River North, and now at his own restaurant, he's a regular in the dining room, stretching tall and thin over the tables with a wide smile in tow. Piccolo Sogno, which translates literally to "little dream," is just that for Priolo and Naples-born business partner Ciro Longobardo. Now, more than a decade later, simple, seasonal and few ingredients, but only the best ones—that's the motto of Italian cookery and what Priolo offers here. Inside a little standalone building, a white marble bar at the front lures guests into the cozy dining room that, during the summer months, flows through open doors to the popular outdoor patio lined with garden beds where Priolo grows fresh herbs and vegetables for use in the kitchen. "We wanted to bring Italy to you," Priolo says of his Tuscany-focused eatery with dishes blended with foods from other Italian regions as well. For his four-cheese ravioli recipe, Priolo suggests looking for the best quality cheeses possible because of the dish's simplicity, and when working with the dough, he recommends using a pasta roller, or a good rolling pin and strong arms.

RAVIOLI QUATTRO FORMAGGI (FOUR CHEESE RAVIOLI)

(SERVES 4, ABOUT 6 PIECES EACH)

For the filling:

1 cup fresh ricotta cheese

2 tablespoons freshly grated Parmigiano Reggiano cheese

2 tablespoons Capriole Farms, locally sourced, or other good-quality goat cheese

2 tablespoons chopped Gorgonzola Dolcelatte cheese

1 teaspoon chopped Italian parsley

Sea salt and freshly ground black pepper, to taste

For the dough:

2¾ cups semolina flour

1¼ cups all-purpose flour

1 teaspoon sea salt

4 egg yolks, plus 1 yolk for egg wash

1 tablespoon olive oil

2 tablespoons water

For the Marsala glaze and sauce:

1 cup Marsala wine

½ cup chicken broth

1 teaspoon heavy cream

2 tablespoons unsalted butter, cut into cubes

Sea salt and freshly ground black pepper, to taste

1 tablespoon toasted pine nuts

Block of Parmigiano Reggiano cheese

To prepare the filling: In a medium bowl, combine the flour, cheeses, parsley, salt and pepper.

To prepare the dough: Place both flours and the salt in a food processor. Add 4 egg yolks and oil; pulse until dough forms a ball. (To prepare by hand, in a large bowl, make a well in the center of dry ingredients. Add 4 yolks and oil to well; using a fork, beat the liquid until smooth and so that it picks up the dry ingredients. Keep mixing until dough forms a ball.)

Knead the dough by hand until slightly firm, similar in feel to your ear lobe. Add water, 1 teaspoon at a time, if dough becomes crumbly or too dry. Rest dough for 10 minutes.

Roll out the dough in one piece using a pasta machine or by hand until the dough is thin enough to see your hand through it. Brush dough with wash made of remaining egg yolk. Drop quarter-size dollops of the cheese filling about 1½ inches apart on one half of the dough. Fold opposite half of the dough over the filled side. Using an inverted shot glass, push down over a mound of filling, pressing air out. With a paring knife, cut around the glass to cut out the ravioli. Press the edges of each ravioli gently to seal. Cover with a damp cloth.

To prepare the Marsala glaze: In a small saucepan over medium-high heat, cook wine until reduced to 2 or 3 tablespoons. Consistency should be thick and syrupy. Set aside.

To prepare the sauce: In a medium saucepan over medium-high heat, reduce the chicken broth by half. Remove from heat, cool slightly, and add the cream and butter, stirring briskly with a wire whisk or fork until sauce is smooth. Season with salt and pepper.

Bring a large pot of water to a boil. Add the ravioli and cook until al dente, about 2 minutes. Drain and toss with sauce.

To serve: Divide ravioli among four plates or shallow bowls. Drizzle with Marsala glaze in a zigzag using a spoon or squirt bottle. Garnish with toasted pine nuts and shavings of Parmigiano Reggiano made using a vegetable peeler.

FORMENTO'S, NONNA'S, THE BRISTOL

925 W Randolph Street
(312) 690-7295
Formentos.com

2152 N Damen Avenue
(773) 862-5555
Thebristolchicago.com

Chef Todd Stein, executive chef/partner for Formento's, Nonna's and The Bristol (B. Hospitality Co.), first became interested in cooking at the young age of 11, when he spent a day shadowing a local restaurant near his hometown of Highland Park in Chicago's northern suburbs. Confirming his passion, he attended Kendall College, later going on to travel and cook around the United States, France and Italy. He started out under the legendary Chef Keith Korn at the former Gordon restaurant and Chef Michael Kornick at mk, later learning how to bake bread at Moulin de la Vierge in France and working as executive chef at David Burke Las Vegas. Stein has also worked at Atlanta's Two Urban Licks, Cleveland's Sans Souci and Vivo, and Minneapolis's BANK. But

Chicago always being his home, he has been working in the city for the past two decades at mk, Cibo Matto, ROOF at the Wit Hotel, The Florentine at the JW Marriot, Piccolo Sogno Due and the restaurants of 4 Star Restaurant Group, earning many accolades over time. It was during his time at Cibo Matto when he came up with his signature duck egg carbonara. Of course, if you don't have any duck eggs on hand, use the freshest chicken eggs you can find, ideally pastured or from a local farm.

DUCK EGG CARBONARA
(SERVES 2)

12 ounces bucatini pasta*

1 tablespoon extra-virgin olive oil

5 ounces pancetta, cut into ¼-inch dice

½ cup freshly grated Pecorino Romano cheese, divided

2 teaspoons cracked black pepper, divided

¼ cup coarsely chopped parsley

2 duck egg yolks

In a large pot of boiling water, cook the pasta until al dente. Drain, reserving 3 tablespoons of the cooking water.

Meanwhile, heat the oil in a large skillet. Add the pancetta and cook over moderate heat until most of the fat has been rendered, about 7 minutes. Add the hot pasta to the skillet and stir to coat, 1 minute. Remove from the heat. Stir in the reserved pasta cooking water, ¼ cup of the grated cheese, and 1 teaspoon of the pepper.

Divide hot pasta evenly between two bowls and sprinkle with the remaining pepper, cheese, and parsley. Place 1 duck egg yolk on top of each pasta dish and serve immediately.

*Bucatini is a spaghetti-like pasta but thicker and with hollow strands. Commonly eaten in Rome, the tubular pasta can be purchased at most grocery stores.

FISK & CO.

225 N Wabash Avenue
(312) 236-9300
Fiskandcochicago.com

Michigan native and Executive Chef at Fisk & Co. Ashlee Aubin first fell in love with the kitchen's high-intensity atmosphere at his first restaurant job as a dishwasher at age 15 in his hometown of Goodrich. Although the job started as a way to earn money for a car, it turned out to be the beginning of his impressive hospitality career. While Ashlee always enjoyed working in restaurants, it took him some time to realize that he wanted to turn his love for cooking into a full-time career. After starting on a path to become a lawyer, he had a change of heart while working at a neighborhood bistro on Chicago's North Side alongside his now fiancée, Chrissy. Their experience working in the kitchen together inspired him to switch gears and pursue a career in the hospitality industry.

Since then, Ashlee has held positions at a variety of notable restaurants in Chicago, including his first four years working up to sous chef at Zealous before getting the opportunity to work with renowned Chef Grant Achatz at Alinea. The next step was opening Wood in Lakeview. After earning accolades, the restaurant team opened Salero, a modern Spanish restaurant in the West Loop, where he earned more accolades. Now, at Fisk & Co., housed in the Kimpton Hotel Monaco, Ashlee remains committed to sourcing local produce and sustainable seafood for the restaurant's Belgian-inspired menu.

When he's not in the kitchen, you can find Ashlee volunteering for organizations like Meals on Wheels or Green City Market, running with his dog Sandy or checking out the city's vibrant art scene and exploring local restaurants in Logan Square and Humboldt Park.

CRAB AND LOBSTER SPAGHETTI
(SERVES 4)

Salt

8 ounces spaghetti (dried or fresh)

1 tablespoon extra-virgin olive oil

1 shallot, minced

2 garlic cloves, minced

1 tablespoon ground Aleppo pepper

½ cup white wine

½ cup heavy cream

6 ounces cooked lobster meat

6 ounces crab meat

½ cup (1 stick) unsalted butter, cubed, chilled

1 tablespoon chopped fresh chives

1 tablespoon chopped parsley

1 lemon, cut into wedges

Bring 4 quarts of water and ¼ cup of salt to a boil in a large pot. If using dried spaghetti, drop it in first and cook until al dente, about 10 minutes.

In a medium saucepan, heat the oil over medium-low heat. Add shallot, garlic, Aleppo and a pinch of salt and cook until fragrant, about 3 minutes.

Add white wine, turn up heat and reduce until almost fully evaporated. Add cream, lobster, crab and a pinch of salt. Turn off heat and add butter, one cube at a time, stirring until thick enough to coat the back of a wooden spoon.

If using fresh pasta, add it to the boiling water. Cook until al dente, about 2 minutes.

Strain the spaghetti and add to the pan with the sauce, tossing with tongs to coat. Divide between bowls, garnish with chopped herbs and lemon wedges and serve.

Daisies

2523 N Milwaukee Avenue
(773) 661-1671
Daisieschicago.com

Chef Joe Frillman named his first restaurant Daisies, partially after his grandmother's nickname, Daisy, who passed away when he was 11 years old, and after the flower that became emblematic for Frillman's wife, Jenna, who lost her mother during college. Hospitality is in both Joe and Jenna Frillman's blood: Joe's great grandmother owned two bars in Chicago, his cousin owns a restaurant and many others in his family are involved in food, while Jenna comes from a restaurant family and the two met while working at The Bristol, for which he was a part of the opening team.

Though Frillman enjoys working with all ingredients, he focuses primarily on plants, sourcing hyper-locally from his brother's farm in Southwest Michigan along the Indiana border. He also has a soft spot for handmade pasta, as in this recipe, after learning the art while traveling in Italy and while working for many years with Chef Rick Tramonto, and later at Balena. "Pasta is a great vessel to utilize scrap products," says Frillman, who's not a fan of food waste; as such, he's known for his pickled vegetables and fermented delicacies, including lacto-fermented sodas and homemade kombucha. Even this recipe wastes not; it uses the entire beet, including the juice, as well as the pressed whey from the ricotta to help thicken the sauce.

AGNOLOTTI WITH ROASTED BEETS AND PICKLED DILL

(MAKES 20 PIECES OF PASTA [2 LARGE OR 4 SMALL SERVINGS])

For the dough:

1,000 grams of all-purpose flour (about 4 cups)

12 egg yolks

6 whole eggs

2 tablespoons (28 grams) water

2 tablespoons (10 grams) kosher salt

For the filling:

2 cups whole milk ricotta

2 cups roasted beets, cut into 2-inch pieces

For the final pasta:

2 ounces reserved whey

2 ounces reserved beet juice

1 tablespoon butter, cubed, chilled

1 large sprig dill, roughly chopped

Sour cream or crème fraîche, for garnish

Poppyseeds and smoked trout roe (or caviar), for garnish (optional)

To prepare the dough: Place flour into a stand mixer fitted with the dough hook. On medium speed, add the eggs and egg yolks, one at a time. Add water and salt, and allow the mixer to knead the dough until well combined, about 20 minutes. Remove dough from the mixer, wrap in plastic wrap, and place in the refrigerator for at least 1 hour.

To prepare the filling: Place beets in a food processor and puree until smooth.

Line a colander with cheesecloth and place over a bowl. Place pureed beets in the center. Cover with

the cheesecloth edges. Place another mixing bowl on top of the beets and set a weight (such as canned food or gallon of milk) in the bowl, pressing to release liquid (this can be done overnight).

Press the cheese using the same method. Line another colander with cheesecloth and place over a bowl. Place ricotta in the center. Cover with the cheesecloth edges and set a weight on the bowl to release liquid.

Save the liquid from the cheese and beets in separate containers and set aside or refrigerate until use when making the pasta sauce.

In a large bowl, mix together the beet puree and ricotta until smooth and transfer to a piping bag or resealable plastic bag with one edge cut out.

To shape and fill the pasta: Using a pasta roller, or a rolling pin, work the prepared pasta dough into thin, long pasta sheets, ⅛ of an inch thick, and 3 inches wide. Using a piping bag or resealable plastic bag with one end cut out, pipe the filling in one continuous line on the bottom edge of the pasta sheet. Carefully fold the sheet over and pinch the dough-covered filling with your index fingers and thumbs, to make stuffed pillow-shaped pouches, with vertical pinched edges. Apply a small amount of water to the remaining top edge of pasta dough using a brush. Using a pasta wheel, cut through the pinched edges of the pouches, to crimp and seal in the filling.

To cook the pasta: Bring a pot of heavily salted water to a boil. Drop in agnolotti and boil until al dente, about 2½ to 3 minutes. Remove using a slotted spoon and set aside.

In a medium saucepan, bring the whey and beet juice to a boil. Reduce by half, turn off heat and allow to cool slightly. Add a tablespoon of the pasta cooking water and butter, stirring until thickened. Fold in pasta and stir to coat.

To serve: Divide pasta among plates. Top each with a sprinkling of dill*, a dollop of sour cream or crème fraîche, and if using, a pinch of poppyseeds and about a teaspoon of smoked trout roe or caviar.

*Make a quick-pickled dill by adding to a jar of pickles or steeping in apple cider vinegar for an extra pop of flavor. This is a great way to store fresh dill that's close to going bad.

saranello's, di pescara

601 N Milwaukee Avenue, Wheeling
(847) 777-6878
Saranellos.com

2124 Northbrook Court, Northbrook
(847) 498-4321
Di-pescara.com

Renowned Chef Mychael Bonner, chef/partner of Lettuce Entertain You Enterprises' Saranello's in Wheeling and Di Pescara in Northbrook, has been with the LEYE family for the past 16 years, and prior to that, served as vice president of culinary operations for Maggiano's for 13 years, during which time he opened 36 locations throughout the country. His experience in food started when he was just a young child watching his mother and grandmother in the kitchen at The Peabody in Memphis. As a high school student in Muncie, Indiana, Bonner began cooking at The Flamingo. He took such a liking to his job that he went on to attend the late Culinary & Hospitality Institute of Chicago (CHIC).

After graduating, Bonner worked as a sous chef at The Signature Room and traveled the country and world, cooking in New York, San Francisco, France and Italy, where he developed a deep passion for handmade pasta. In 2011, Bonner worked with partner Mark Tormey to open Saranello's. "With the menu, I feel like I can truly connect with the food because we are literally making these pastas daily by hand every day," he says. His recipe for spinach and ricotta gnocchi is easy to make without the fuss of kneading, and it pairs well with a bright green, classic pesto. His tomato and summer squash gratin—a favorite from his childhood when his mom made the dish for him—is a great way to use up extra produce or finds from the farmers market during the summer season. Bonner remains passionate about working local farms and bringing fresh food to the greater public; he sources a large bulk of the produce for his kitchen from Urban Growers Collective, a Chicago-based non-profit and urban agriculture project dedicated to cultivating nourishing environments that support health, economic development, healing and creativity.

SPINACH AND RICOTTA GNOCCHI
(SERVES 10)

For the gnocchi:

3 cups spinach, washed and dried*

1¼ pounds ricotta, drained

1 egg yolk

1 cup freshly grated Parmesan or Parmigiano Reggiano cheese

1 cup fresh breadcrumbs

1 teaspoon salt

¼ teaspoon freshly ground black pepper

½ teaspoon ground nutmeg

8 ounces all-purpose flour

For the pesto:

Makes 7½ cups

2 cloves fresh garlic

4 cups fresh basil, lightly packed, plus more for garnish

¼ cup lightly toasted pine nuts

⅛ teaspoon salt, or to taste

¼ teaspoon freshly ground black pepper, or to taste

½ cup extra-virgin olive oil

½ cup freshly grated Parmesan or Parmigiano Reggiano cheese, plus more for garnish

To begin preparing the gnocchi: Bring a medium pot of water to a boil. Add spinach and cook until very tender, about 5 minutes. Transfer immediately to an ice bath. When cool, drain and transfer spinach to a food processor. Pulse until very smooth.

Line a colander with cheesecloth and place over a medium or large mixing bowl. Pour puree into the center and drain for 30 minutes.

To prepare the pesto: Combine the garlic, basil, pine nuts and salt and pepper in a food processor and pulse until the ingredients are roughly chopped. With the motor running, pour in the olive oil until well-incorporated. Transfer the sauce to a mixing bowl and add the cheese. Pesto will keep in the refrigerator, covered, for up to 10 days.

To continue the gnocchi: Wring out any excess liquid from the spinach and transfer to a large bowl. Add the ricotta, egg yolk, Parmesan, breadcrumbs, salt, pepper and nutmeg, mixing with your hands to combine.

Spoon the flour into the spinach mixture, a little bit at a time, until the flour is fully incorporated, gently mixing with your hands until a ball forms.

Place the mixture into a pastry bag or resealable plastic bag with one edge cut out. Dust a preparation area with flour and pipe out the spinach mixture in a single row. Cut into 1-inch logs.

In a large pot of boiling, salted water, cook gnocchi until they float to the top, about 2 to 4 minutes, using a slotted spoon to remove pieces one by one when ready, placing in a mixing bowl.

Gently toss gnocchi with enough pesto sauce to coat. Divide pasta among bowls, garnish with extra Parmesan and fresh basil and serve warm.

*Use frozen, thawed spinach and skip the boiling process for faster preparation. Proceed with the straining instructions.

TOMATO AND SUMMER SQUASH GRATIN
(SERVES 4)

¼ cup extra-virgin olive oil

3 medium yellow onions, diced

4 cloves garlic, minced

2 medium sized tomatoes, grated, or 1 (8-ounce) can tomato puree or sauce

3 tablespoons fresh basil, roughly chopped, plus more for garnish

½ cup plus 2 tablespoons grated Parmesan cheese, divided

¼ teaspoon freshly ground black pepper

2 tablespoons softened butter

3 to 4 medium zucchini, sliced into ¼-inch-thick rounds

3 to 4 medium-to-small yellow squash, sliced into ¼-inch-thick rounds

4 medium ripe tomatoes, sliced into ¼-inch-thick rounds

Preheat oven to 350°F.

Using a large, heavy bottom sauté pan, heat olive oil over medium-low heat. Add onions and cook until soft and golden brown, about 30 minutes, stirring occasionally. Add garlic and cook until fragrant, about 3 to 4 minutes.

Add grated tomato or tomato puree and cook until moisture reduces by half. Stir in basil and cook until most of the moisture has evaporated. Stir in ½ cup Parmesan cheese and pepper. Mixture should be thick with little to no excess moisture.

Butter a 9-inch glass or ceramic baking dish. Spoon sauce into the dish, using a wooden spoon or spatula to spread it out in an even layer. Working from left to right, layer the sliced vegetables by making one row of zucchini placed tightly together from one end to the other. Repeat this step using the sliced tomatoes, making sure to slightly overlap with the zucchini next to it. Make another row using the yellow squash. Repeat with remaining slices until the whole dish is covered. Sprinkle remaining Parmesan cheese over all.

Cover with parchment paper and then with aluminum foil. Bake for 20 to 25 minutes, or until vegetables are soft. Remove from the oven and let the dish rest for 10 minutes.

Garnish with more basil, if desired, and serve warm.

La Luna Chicago, Tree House

1726 S Racine Avenue
(312) 248-8957
Lalunachicago.com

149 W Kinzie Street
(773) 348-8899
Treehousechicago.com

Chef Marco Colin oversees the culinary operations at La Luna Chicago and Tree House, the latter of which opened most recently in March 2021. Colin, who was recruited by Sam Sanchez, CEO of Third Coast Hospitality Group and his two daughters, Samantha Sanchez, CEO of La Luna Chicago and Korina Sanchez, general counsel, elevates typical comfort food with a high quality, ingredient-focused approach to modern Italian fare. The kitchen's two ovens, a custom-built, wood-burning brick oven and traditional deck oven, serve up Tree House's three styles of pizza. Here Colin offers a recipe for rigatoni with vodka sauce, a classic Italian-American dish. "It's one of my favorite recipes to make and eat. When I eat it, it makes me feel happy and warm," he says. "It's just too good and easy to make. All my family and friends love when I make it." For a meatless version, simply skip the prosciutto.

RIGATONI WITH CRISPY PROSCIUTTO AND VODKA SAUCE

(SERVES 4-6)

3 tablespoons unsalted butter

½ cup chopped prosciutto (optional)

1 shallot, minced

2 cloves garlic, minced

½ cup tomato paste

½ teaspoon crushed red pepper flakes

2 tablespoons vodka

Kosher salt, to taste

1 pound rigatoni

½ cup heavy cream

½ cup freshly grated Parmesan, plus more for garnish

2 pinches ground nutmeg

½ cup chopped chives or torn basil leaves, for garnish

Melt 1 tablespoon of the butter in a large skillet over medium heat. Add prosciutto and fry until crispy and fat has rendered, stirring once or twice, about 6 minutes. Remove using a slotted spoon and let drain on a paper towel-lined plate.

Add remaining butter, shallot and garlic and cook until fragrant and softened, stirring frequently, 4 to 5 minutes.

Add tomato paste and red pepper flakes and cook, stirring frequently, until paste has coated shallots and garlic is beginning to darken, about 5 minutes.

Add vodka, scraping up any browned bits with a wooden spoon. Once alcohol has burned off, about 1 minute, turn off heat.

Bring a large pot of salted water to a boil and cook pasta until al dente. Reserve 2 cups of pasta water before draining.

Return sauce to medium heat and add ¼ cup of pasta water and heavy cream, stirring to combine. Add half the Parmesan and the nutmeg and stir until melted. Turn off heat and stir in cooked pasta. Fold in remaining Parmesan, adding more pasta water (about a tablespoon at a time) if the sauce is looking dry. Season with salt if needed. Serve with extra Parmesan, chopped chives or torn basil leaves, if desired.

FISH

It's 5 a.m. and the sun's nowhere in sight. Cutting through the cold darkness, trucks loaded with the day's freshest catch make their way through the quiet streets of the meatpacking district, the former home of the stockyards infamously described in Upton Sinclair's *The Jungle*, which today has become the West Loop restaurant mecca, home to Chicago's top dining destinations. A brave resident here or there shuffles in and out of the wholesaler warehouses, carrying mesh bags full of shrimp and lobsters packed on ice. The rest of the loot will go off to the restaurants come daybreak.

Historically, Chicago is a meat town. But thanks to O'Hare International Airport's status as one of the largest and busiest airports in the U.S., Chicago has easy access to fish flown in daily from all parts of the world.

Cold-water oysters on the half shell, jumbo shrimp cocktail, whole lobsters with drawn butter, and Parmesan-crusted, baked clams. Seafood has a long history in Chicago, starting at the steakhouses in the 1920s and '30s and later, at Italian restaurants looking to incorporate shellfish in big bowls of homemade pasta.

Now, fresh fish is everywhere in Chicago, from sushi powerhouses to the neighborhood restaurant down the block. What's shared among most of Chicago, these days, is a commitment to sourcing sustainable seafood and eschewing anything but. The unintended benefit of that, for diners, is being able to enjoy the freshest, healthiest fish possible.

PROXI

565 W Randolph Street
(312) 466-1950
Proxichicago.com

After nearly 10 years of a successful run with Sepia, Chef Andrew Zimmerman and Restaurateur Emmanuel Nony opened their second concept, Proxi, a bustling, energetic restaurant just down the street with a focus on global cuisine and addictive cocktails. The duo continues to operate their finer dining outpost but have expanded upon their business by also opening a private dining and event space connected to the back of it (that's seen many a hopping party). "A lot of the dishes we do start off at least inspired by classic, rustic cooking and then we take a contemporary approach to it," says Zimmerman. "We're also committed to trying to use as much sustainable, seasonal, local, and organic product as we can." In this bass recipe, the simple and sweet corn chowder reflects the flavors of the Midwest.

WILD STRIPED BASS WITH SWEET CORN CHOWDER AND LITTLENECK CLAMS
(SERVES 4)

4 ears sweet corn, kernels removed

2 leeks, white part only, diced

3 stalks celery heart, chopped

2 medium carrots, peeled and diced

1 medium onion, diced

4 sprigs fresh thyme

1 bay leaf

¼ cup plus 1 tablespoon extra-virgin olive oil, divided

1½ pounds young potatoes (fingerling, German butterball), chopped

16 pearl onions, peeled

2 cups heavy cream, reduced to 1 cup

12 littleneck clams, scrubbed

¼ cup chopped flat-leaf parsley

Salt and freshly ground black pepper

4 6-ounce fillets wild-caught striped bass, skin on

Reserve ¼ cup of the corn kernels for garnish. In a large stockpot, combine half of the leeks, celery, carrots, and diced onion, plus ½ cup corn kernels, 2 sprigs thyme, and the bay leaf. Pour in enough cold water to cover by about 2 inches and bring to a boil. Reduce heat and simmer 40 minutes.

Strain the corn broth, discarding the solids. Wash out the stockpot and heat 1 tablespoon oil over medium heat. Add the remaining leeks, celery, carrots, and diced onion, and the remaining corn kernels. Season with a pinch of salt and cook until onions are soft and translucent, about 2-3 minutes.

Add the corn broth, remaining 2 sprigs thyme, potatoes, pearl onions, and cream. Simmer chowder until potatoes are tender, about 20 minutes. Add the clams and continue to cook until shells just begin to open. Add the parsley and season with salt and pepper as needed.

Heat the remaining ¼ cup oil in a large sauté pan over medium-high heat. Season the bass with salt and pepper and cook, skin side down, about 4-5 minutes, or until skin is crispy and golden. Flip fillets and continue to cook until opaque and just cooked through, another 2-3 minutes.

To serve: Scoop the chowder vegetables and clams evenly into four shallow bowls. Pour in broth and top each bowl with a bass fillet, skin side up. Garnish with remaining ¼ cup corn kernels.

GT FISH & OYSTER

531 N Wells Street
(312) 929-3501
Gtoyster.com

When the first edition of this cookbook was released, Chef Giuseppe Tentori, then the executive chef of Boka, had just opened his own namesake restaurant with the Boka Restaurant Group: GT Fish & Oyster, a modern seafood restaurant that opened in 2011. Since then, Tentori and the restaurant have earned many accolades, including a Michelin star and a finalist for the James Beard "Best Chef: Great Lakes" award. He later went on to open GT Prime, a modern steakhouse restaurant, just down the street. Both restaurants have been busy hotspots over the years taking up residence in the Near North section of downtown. In addition, Tentori serves as the executive chef of Boka Catering Group. Here, Tentori offers the clam chowder that he took months to perfect, first serving the soup at Boka and then making it the star of his seafood concept. Tentori uses diamondback clams from New Zealand for their meaty texture and umami taste, dropping them into the simmering stock just before serving to prevent rubberiness from overcooking. For this recipe, though, any whole clams may be used.

GT'S CLAM CHOWDER
(SERVES 4, EACH PORTION 8 OUNCES)

3 ounces diced bacon

7 ounces chopped onion

4 ounces chopped celery

1 ounce chopped garlic

6 ounces white wine, divided

10 ounces clam juice

12 ounces heavy cream

5 sprigs fresh thyme

1 bay leaf

1 pound diced Yukon Gold potatoes

2 tablespoons cornstarch

2 tablespoons cold water

2 pounds whole clams

1 tablespoon butter

1 tablespoon extra-virgin olive oil

1 tablespoon chopped shallot

Salt and freshly ground black pepper, to taste

Chopped fresh chives, for garnish

Dash Tabasco sauce or other hot pepper sauce

Cook bacon in a large saucepan over medium heat 5 minutes. Add onion, celery, and garlic and cook 1 minute. Add 3 ounces wine; reduce until the alcohol has cooked off, about 2 minutes. Add clam juice, heavy cream, thyme sprigs, and bay leaf; bring slowly to a simmer.

Add potatoes and cook at a low simmer over medium-low heat for 15 minutes. Do not boil or soup will break. In a small bowl, mix cornstarch and water until smooth, and stir mixture into soup. Simmer until thickened to a chowder consistency. Discard thyme sprigs and bay leaf and set pan aside.

Wash clams thoroughly, making sure to rid them of any residual sand. Melt butter with olive oil in a large sauté pan over medium heat. Add shallot and cook 1 minute. Add remaining 3 ounces wine and bring to a simmer. Add clams and cook for about 5 minutes, or until shells open. Gently stir clam mixture into the chowder. Season chowder with salt and pepper to taste.

To serve: Ladle into four bowls. Garnish with chives and Tabasco sauce and serve with a crusty baguette.

GIRL & THE GOAT, LITTLE GOAT, DUCK DUCK GOAT, CABRA CEVICHERIA

809 W Randolph Street
(312) 492-6262
Girlandthegoat.com

820 W Randolph Street
(312) 888-3455
Littlegoatchicago.com

857 W Fulton Market
(312) 902-3825
Duckduckgoatchicago.com

200 N Green Street
(312) 761-1717
Cabrachicago.com

Celebrity Chef Stephanie Izard celebrated the 10-year anniversary of Girl & The Goat in 2021. During the past decade, the Bravo TV's *Top Chef* Season 4 (and first female chef) winner and "Iron Chef" star, through her partnership with Boka Restaurant Group, has expanded her empire to include Little Goat, a more casual diner across the street as well as Duck Duck Goat, a Chinese-inspired concept in the West Loop that has a cult following for her Peking duck.

Most recently, she opened Cabra Cevicheria, a Peruvian concept, on the rooftop of the hot new Hoxton hotel in 2019, and she plans to open a second Girl & The Goat location in Los Angeles. Izard has earned countless awards and accolades since her launch into the public eye following the Top Chef win, including Best Chef: Great Lakes in 2011 and 2013. During the global pandemic of 2021, Izard launched a to-go bakery concept, and she continues to offer catering through Little Goat. Her Mighty Goat sausage is a signature one and reflective of her trademark, which hails from her last name, which refers to a type of mountain goat from the Pyrenees mountain range. If goat meat is less preferred taste-wise or hard to come by, substitute lamb.

MUSSELS WITH MIGHTY GOAT SAUSAGE, CILANTRO BUTTER, AND BAGNA CAUDA AIOLI

(SERVES 4-6; MAKES ABOUT 1 POUND SAUSAGE)

For the Mighty Goat sausage:

½ pound goat meat, cubed (substitute lamb if goat is unavailable)

1½ ounces pork meat, cubed

1½ ounces pork fatback, cubed

Salt and freshly ground black pepper, to taste

1 teaspoon ground mustard seed

1 teaspoon ground fennel seed

½ teaspoon ground cardamom

½ clove garlic

1½ teaspoons chopped shallots

¼ cup chopped fennel bulb

1 tablespoon white wine

½ tablespoon water

2 teaspoons tamarind paste

2 tablespoons chopped cilantro

For the cilantro butter:

2 cloves garlic

¼ cup chopped cilantro

½ cup butter (1 stick)

Grated zest of 1 orange

½ teaspoon cayenne pepper

For the bagna cauda aioli:

2 egg yolks

1 tablespoon Dijon mustard

1 tablespoon sherry vinegar

1 cup vegetable oil

3 anchovy fillets

3 large garlic cloves, chopped

Salt, to taste

For the mussels:

1 tablespoon olive oil

¼ cup finely chopped shallots

1 pound mussels, cleaned

⅔ cup Goose Island Sofie ale, or other Belgian-style ale

Crushed red pepper, to taste

Salt, to taste

1 cup croutons, packaged or homemade

To prepare the Mighty Goat sausage: Place the goat meat, pork, and pork fatback on a sheet tray and freeze until cold but not frozen. Season the meat with salt, pepper, mustard seed, fennel seed, and cardamom.

Using a stand mixer fitted with a meat grinder attachment, grind the meat, garlic, shallot, and fennel together into the mixing bowl. On medium speed, emulsify the meat with the wine, water, and tamarind using the paddle attachment, about 3-4 minutes. Cook a small bit of sausage to check for seasoning and adjust if necessary. Mix in the cilantro on low speed until fully incorporated. Cover meat and refrigerate. (This can be made a day ahead.)

To prepare the cilantro butter: In a food processor or blender, blend the garlic and cilantro together until smooth. Add the butter, cube by cube, until well combined and aerated. Add the orange zest and cayenne pepper and continue mixing until blended and aerated.

To prepare the bagna cauda aioli: In a blender, combine egg yolks, mustard, and vinegar. On medium-high speed, slowly pour the oil in to emulsify and thicken. When emulsified, add the anchovies and garlic and blend until smooth. Season with salt to taste, cover, and refrigerate.

To prepare the mussels: In a large pot with a lid, heat the olive oil and cook shallots over medium heat for 4 minutes. Add goat sausage and cook, breaking up into small pieces, about 3-4 minutes or until slightly browned.

Add the mussels and beer. Cover and steam mussels until all mussels are open, about 2-3 minutes. Discard any mussels that do not open. Add cilantro butter and cook until melted. Season with crushed red pepper and salt. Add croutons and toss to coat and moisten.

To serve: Transfer mussels to serving bowls. Drizzle bagna cauda aioli over the mussels.

LULA CAFÉ, MARISOL

2537 N Kedzie Boulevard
(773) 489-9554
Lulacafe.com

205 E Pearson Street
(312) 799-3599
Marisolchicago.com (Temporarily closed)

Lula Café in the heart of Logan Square has served as the beacon for vegetarians and plant-centric eaters for more than two decades. The restaurant, which opened in a tiny storefront in 1999, expanded to serve meat (and cocktails) a while back now, and it's gone through a couple major renovations. That's helped the restaurant stay fresh as Jason Hammel has ventured into other concepts as well, opening Marisol at the Contemporary Museum of Art in 2017 and partnering with

Chefs Yoshi Yamada and Zeeshan Shah to open Superkhana International (p. 124). Hammel is also well known for being a pioneer in Chicago's local food movement back in the late 1990s and early 2000s. He was one of the first to connect local farmers with chefs in Chicago and even elsewhere around the country.

Hammel also remains dedicated to various charities, including Pilot Light, a non-profit organization which he co-founded, dedicated to educating local students on the importance of making healthy food choices. The organization celebrated its 10th anniversary in 2020. For this elegant fish dish, "white asparagus can be a good choice in the spring when you're impatient for green, tired of root vegetables and looking for something bright, acidic and crunchy to put you in an elevated mood," he says. While sous-vide cooking is often used for a dish like this at the restaurant, at home, basting the fish imitates the gentle and constant heat and moisture of a water bath. The poached liquid can be prepared ahead and stored in the refrigerator for a few days. He suggests storing white asparagus in water with a halved lemon to prevent oxidation.

MILK-POACHED COD WITH WHITE ASPARAGUS AND CHARRED PIQUILLO PEPPERS

(SERVES 4)

For the poaching liquid, cod, and piquillo peppers:

2 tablespoons unsalted butter

2 fennel bulbs, cored and thinly sliced

1 cup Pernod, absinthe, or anise-flavored liqueur (such as Herbsaint)

½ cup sugar

1 cup chicken stock or low-sodium broth

1 cup whole milk

¼ teaspoon salt

4 5-ounce cod fillets

1 8-ounce can piquillo peppers, drained

For the asparagus salad:

1 bunch white asparagus, bottom ends trimmed, and stalks peeled

¼ cup sugar

½ cup lemon juice

½ cup extra-virgin olive oil

2 tablespoons champagne vinegar

1 bulb fennel, cored and shaved using a vegetable peeler

½ tablespoon chopped fresh dill

To prepare the poaching liquid: In a heavy-bottomed saucepan, melt the butter over medium heat. Add fennel and cook until caramelized, about 5 minutes. Reduce heat to medium-low if butter begins to brown too fast. Add the Pernod, sugar, and stock or broth. Bring to a boil, then turn off heat immediately, allowing to cool slightly. Stir in milk, season with salt, and cool completely. Set aside.

To prepare the asparagus salad: Blanch asparagus in salted boiling water until just tender. Transfer to an ice bath. Drain, slice into ¼-inch-thick pieces, and set aside. In a large bowl, mix together the sugar, lemon juice, oil, and vinegar. Fold in asparagus, shaved fennel, and dill. Refrigerate.

Blister the piquillo peppers on an open flame or in a broiler. Cut into ½-inch-thick slices. Set aside.

To prepare the cod: Bring the poaching liquid back up to a simmer over medium-high heat. Reduce heat to medium, bringing liquid down to a gentle simmer. Carefully add fillets and poach until fish is opaque and just cooked through, about 3 minutes.

To serve: Add a spoonful of the sliced piquillo peppers, warmed in the microwave for 10-20 seconds. Place a cod fillet over the peppers. Ladle about 1 ounce of the poaching liquid over the fish. Serve with asparagus salad in individual, chilled bowls.

WISCONSIN TROUT SOUP WITH POTATO-INFUSED CREAM AND BACON

(SERVES 4)

For the soup:

3 slices bacon, diced

1 small yellow onion, chopped

1 celery rib, chopped

½ bulb fennel, cored, chopped

Salt and pepper

1 head garlic, cloves peeled and thinly sliced

½ teaspoon tomato paste

1 cup dry white wine

Splash of orange juice

Splash of apple cider (optional)

1 12-14-ounce smoked trout fillet

4 cups fish, chicken, or vegetable stock or low-sodium broth

¼ cup chopped fresh chives, divided

1 cup sour cream or crème fraîche

For the potato cream and cheese garnish:

1 cup heavy cream

3 small fingerling or other starchy potatoes about the size of an index finger

½ cup grated Wisconsin or other artisanal, good-quality sharp cheddar cheese

To prepare the soup: In a heavy-bottomed non-aluminum pot over low heat, cook the bacon pieces until some of the fat has rendered but pieces are not crisp, about 2-3 minutes. Transfer bacon pieces with a slotted spoon to paper towels; set aside.

Turn heat up to medium. Add the onion, celery, and fennel and cook until vegetables are soft and translucent but not browned, stirring constantly, about 2 minutes. Season with salt and pepper. Add the garlic and cook until fragrant, 30 seconds. Add the tomato paste and continue to stir, 30 seconds. Pour in the wine, orange juice, and apple cider if using, stirring to combine. Cook until liquid has fully reduced, and mixture is dry. Add the trout flesh and head, stock, and half of the chives.

Bring mixture to a gentle simmer. Continue to simmer, uncovered, skimming foam, not the fat, off the surface several times.

To prepare the potato cream garnish: Heat the cream in a small saucepan over medium heat. Bundle the potatoes in a cheesecloth and submerge in the cream. Continue to cook until cream reduces by a third and is thick enough to coat the back of a spoon. Using a wooden spoon, smash the potatoes slightly. Remove the potato bundle and set aside. Transfer saucepan with the cream to an off burner. Whisk in a touch of water if cream becomes gluey.

Soup will be ready when broth is clearer, mildly salty and fishy in taste but smooth and rich, about 45 minutes to 1 hour. Remove from heat, allow to cool slightly. Add the sour cream or crème fraîche and stir constantly to thicken, about 3 minutes.

Transfer soup to a blender in small batches and puree until smooth. Alternatively, puree soup using an immersion blender. Strain soup several times through a very fine strainer until almost smooth. Soup will still have a slightly chalky consistency.

To serve: Divide among four bowls. Drizzle each with the warm potato cream. Remove potatoes from bundle; roughly chop. Garnish with chopped potatoes, bacon, remaining chives, and cheddar cheese, if desired.

THE DEARBORN

145 N Dearborn Street
(312) 384-1242
Thedearborntavern.com

Chef Aaron Cuschieri has served as executive chef of The Dearborn since 2016, when he helped launch the vision for the urban American tavern with owners Clodagh and Amy Lawless.

A Detroit native, Cuschieri attended culinary school at the Art Institute of Michigan and began cooking at Assaggi Bistro in Ferndale, Michigan, where he rose from sous chef to executive chef within a year. He then staged and was hired at Chicago's acclaimed Alinea.

Cuschieri soon was tapped by Chef Takashi Yagihashi to be chef de cuisine at Takashi restaurant, which led him to the executive chef position at Yagihashi's second restaurant, Slurping Turtle. In 2015, Cuschieri began running the kitchen at Kinmont, where, under the tutelage of Chef Jared Van Camp, he channeled the restaurant's sustainable "Field & Stream" ethos into eclectic menu items like the fish-focused charcuterie board.

At The Dearborn, Cuschieri draws from the agricultural bounty of his native Midwest in a kitchen of his own creativity, merging his fine-dining experience with a genuine, unpretentious appreciation for food. He has earned multiple accolades and has appeared on a variety of TV shows, including Season 11 of Bravo's popular *Top Chef* series (2013, New Orleans) and the Food Network's "Beat Bobby Flay" (2019). This is a simple yet seasonally delicious seafood dish; if ramps are not in season, you can substitute large scallions or green garlic. You can also use English or sweet peas instead of fava beans for the smash.

GRILLED SWORDFISH STEAK WITH FAVA BEAN SMASH, GRILLED RAMP VINAIGRETTE, DATES, FRISÉE AND HEARTS OF PALM SALAD

(SERVES 2)

For the swordfish:

2 (10- to 12-ounce) oz swordfish steaks

¼ cup canola or neutral oil

Salt

Freshly ground black pepper

For the fava smash:

2 cups fava beans, shucked and peeled

2 tablespoons extra-virgin olive oil

2 teaspoons salt, plus more for boiling

2 teaspoons freshly ground black pepper

For the ramp vinaigrette:

20 fresh ramps

1 cup plus 1 tablespoon olive oil, divided

2 teaspoons salt

1 teaspoon freshly ground black pepper

2 tablespoons Dijon mustard

¼ cup champagne vinegar

For the salad:

2 heads frisée lettuce

½ bulb fennel, thinly sliced or shaved

3 pieces hearts of palm, sliced into ¼-inch rings

10 each pitted dates, chopped

½ lemon

1 tablespoon extra-virgin olive oil

To prepare the fava smash: Bring a medium saucepan filled with salted water to a boil. Add fava beans and cook until soft, about 4 to 5 minutes. Drain and transfer to a mortar.

Add the oil, salt and black pepper. Use a pestle to lightly mash the fava beans. The mixture should be chunky and slightly creamy. Alternatively, blend the mixture in a food processor. Set aside.

Heat a charcoal or gas grill to hot.

To prepare the vinaigrette: Rub ramps with 1 tablespoon of the olive oil and season with salt and black pepper. Grill ramps on very hot grill until charred, about 2 to 3 minutes. Set aside.

To prepare the swordfish: Rub swordfish with oil and season with salt and pepper. Place swordfish on the hot side of the grill and cook until browned on the outside and opaque in the center, flipping once, about 10 to 12 minutes. Remove from grill and set aside.

Once cool enough to handle, chop the ramps. Place the grilled ramps, mustard and vinegar in a food processor and pulse until smooth and chunky. Slowly pour in remaining oil while pulsing. Season to taste with salt and black pepper.

To prepare the salad: Mix together the lettuce, fennel, hearts of palm and dates. Drizzle with olive and then the juice from the lemon. Toss to combine.

To serve: Divide fava smash evenly between two plates and top each with a swordfish steak. Drizzle 2 ounces of ramp sauce over each plate. Divide salad between the plates and serve immediately.

OSTERIA LANGHE

2824 W Armitage Avenue
(773) 661-1582
Osterialanghe.com

As head chef and partner of the beloved Logan Square restaurant focused on the Piedmont region of Italy, Chef Cameron Grant actually hails from Edinburgh, Scotland originally before moving to Boulder, Colorado with his family at the age of 12. His love for Italian food runs deep, however, having worked under acclaimed Chef Sakima Isaac at Laudisio Restante Italiano in Boulder and later taking an externship during culinary school to Treiso, Italy, where he staged at the Michelin-starred restaurant La Ciau del Tornavento under Chef Maurilio Garola. While there, Grant learned the art of Piedmontese cooking and the value of using local fresh ingredients from nearby farms.

Following the completion of his externship in 2005, Grant returned to the States and Laudisio as sous chef before quickly climbing the ranks to becoming executive chef of the restaurant. A few years later, the opportunity arose for Grant to open his own restaurant in Treiso, Italy with an old friend and new partner Guillermo Field Melendez down the road from where they had met at La Ciau del Tornavento. Together they opened Profumo di Vino in 2008, a contemporary restaurant and wine bar serving seasonal Piedmontese cuisine in a casual setting. In 2010, Grant sold his share of the Profumo di Vino and moved back to the States, eventually landing in the Chicago area when he accepted the executive chef role to open Fresco 21 at the Intercontinental O'Hare Hotel. In 2013, Grant was introduced to Italian wine expert Aldo Zaninotto while he dined at Fresco 21, and the two sparked a friendship over his knack for cooking authentic Italian dishes. A year later, the two joined forces to open Osteria Langhe, a Piedmontese-focused restaurant in Chicago's Logan Square neighborhood. This risotto dish is one that he learned while working in Piedmont. "It's very simple, approachable and delicious," says Grant of the shrimp, tomato, cream, butter and Parmigiano Reggiano combination. It just takes a little extra attention and TLC to make. You can roast the onion for the extra side or starter while stirring the risotto.

RISOTTO CERTOSINO
(SERVES 2-4)

12 to 24 (16/20 size) peeled, deveined shrimp, tail on

1 tablespoon extra-virgin olive oil, plus more for garnish

2 tablespoons diced onion

1 cup carnarolli (or arborio) rice

2 tablespoons white wine

4 tablespoons heavy cream

12 ounces hot chicken stock

½ cup canned, crushed tomatoes

¼ teaspoon dried oregano, or to taste, plus more for garnish

Salt, to taste

Freshly ground black pepper, to taste

2 tablespoons Parmigiano Reggiano, plus more for garnish

1½ tablespoon unsalted butter

To serve 6 shrimps per person, if making risotto for 2, set aside 4 whole shrimp and remove the tail and roughly chop the remaining shrimps. If serving 4, set aside 8 whole shrimp and chop 4 of the shrimp into ½-inch pieces.

Heat oil in a small saucepot over medium heat.

When oil is sizzling, add the onion and cook until soft and translucent, about 2 minutes. Add the rice, stirring to sear it in the hot oil with a wooden spoon. Continuously stir to prevent browning (this step ensures that the individual rice kernels stay intact during cooking and prevents gumminess).

Add wine, stirring to break up browned bits, until alcohol burns off, about 1 minute. Reduce heat to medium-low and add cream, tomatoes and oregano.

In a separate, small saucepot, bring stock to a boil, then reduce heat and maintain a gentle simmer.

Add a 2- to 3-ounce ladleful of the hot stock to the pot with the rice. Season with a pinch each of salt and pepper. Continue to stir regularly, allowing the stock to reduce before adding more. Once most of the stock is absorbed, taste for seasoning and adjust as needed. The rice will take about 18 minutes to cook from start to finish and when fully cooked, will have a little bite and no stickiness.

Add the diced and whole shrimp and cook until pink, about 1 minute, being careful not to overcook them.

Take risotto off heat and stir in the butter and Parmigiano Reggiano. Remove the whole shrimp and place to the side.

Divide the risotto evenly between bowls and garnish with the reserved whole shrimp (2 per bowl), and if desired, a sprinkling of dried oregano, extra Parmigiano Reggiano, minced chives or parsley, and/or a drizzle of extra-virgin olive oil. Serve warm.

CIPOLLA ARROSTO
(SERVES 2)

1 large yellow onion (skin on)

2 teaspoons olive oil, divided, plus more for garnish

2 pinches salt, divided

2 ounces pancetta, diced

2 ounces grated Parmigiano Reggiano cheese

2 pinches freshly ground black pepper

2 tablespoons heavy cream

2 sprigs thyme, leaves removed

1 egg yolk, plus a little egg white

Arugula

3 grape tomatoes

4 Amaretto cookies, crumbled (optional)

Preheat the oven to 350°F.

Place the onion on a sheet or baking tray and coat with 1 teaspoon of the olive oil. Season with salt and roast until tender when lightly squeezed, about 20 to 30 minutes. Transfer to the refrigerator to chill.

Heat 1 teaspoon of olive oil in a small pan over medium heat. Add pancetta and cook until crispy and fat is rendered.

Remove the onion from the fridge and slice in half. Remove the interior onion flesh, leaving one layer of cooked onion inside the roasted skin for structure and to create a cup for the filling.

Cut the removed roasted onion into thin strips and place in a small bowl. Season with a pinch of salt and the pepper.

Add the cream, egg, ¾ of the Parmigiano-Reggiano, thyme leaves and ¾ of the crispy pancetta. Mix well.

Fill onion cups with the onion mixture. Turn oven up to 375°F and bake until internal temperature of one the onion cups reads 145°F, about 10 to 15 minutes.

To serve: Place a handful of arugula on each of 2 serving plates. Top each with 3 grape tomato halves, about 1 teaspoon olive oil and a pinch each of salt and pepper. Top with the roasted onion cup. Sprinkle crushed amaretto cookies around the edges, if desired. Garnish with remaining Parmigiano Reggiano and crispy pancetta.

THE GRACEFUL ORDINARY

3 E Main Street, St. Charles
(331) 235-5803
Thegracefulordinary.com

Chris Curren spent nearly two decades heading up the kitchens of top restaurants in Chicago and Cleveland, becoming a fixture on the Midwestern culinary scene, before opening up his latest restaurant in 2021 in the suburbs with his wife Megan. An Ohio native, after graduating from the Pennsylvania Culinary Institute in 2002, Curren and went on to hone his professional skills in Cleveland-area kitchens under the influential Chef Bruce Kalman and at top spots including celebrated contemporary American restaurant Three Birds. After relocating to Chicago in 2006, Curren opened critically renowned fine-dining concept Blue 13, which would garner recognition in the prestigious Michelin guide and earned him Jean Banchet Award nominations in both the Rising Star Chef and Best Fine Dining categories in 2011. Curren led culinary operations at some of the city's top hospitality collectives, serving as corporate executive chef at Fifty/50 Restaurant Group and later executive chef at acclaimed sommelier Alpana Singh's Seven Lions in the Loop and at West Loop hotspot Fulton Market Kitchen. Curren says mussels are his go-to comfort food, especially on a cold day. "This particular recipe has an extremely flavorful broth that can be slopped up with a bit of warm, crusty bread and it really feeds both your stomach and your soul," he says. "It's also a fairly basic recipe that can easily be done by the average home cook and is very forgiving if it is not done perfectly. Even if you make some mistakes, you still end up with a great dish."

STEAMED MUSSELS WITH LOBSTER BUTTER SAUCE
(SERVES 2-4)

For the mussels:

2 tablespoons olive oil

2 pounds fresh mussels (such as PEI or green-lipped)

2 teaspoons minced garlic

2 teaspoons minced shallots

Pinch red chili flakes

½ cup white wine

For the lobster butter*:

(Makes 1 pound)

1 pound unsalted butter, softened

2¾ teaspoons minced garlic

3 teaspoons minced parsley

½ teaspoon dried basil

½ teaspoon dried thyme

1 teaspoon minced chives, plus more for garnish (optional)

2 teaspoons Dijon mustard

2 teaspoons paprika

3 ounces lobster stock base (such as Minor's or Better Than Bouillon)

To prepare the lobster butter: Combine all the ingredients for the lobster butter in a stand mixer and mix on medium-low speed (or whisk vigorously by hand) until all ingredients are fully incorporated. Reserve 3 ounces (about 6 tablespoons) of the butter and refrigerate or freeze the rest for later use.

To prepare the mussels: Check if any mussels are open or have cracks in their shell. Tap any open mussels on the counter and discard if they do not close. Discard mussels with large cracks in their shell.

Heat oil in a large sauté pan over high heat for about 1 minute. Remove the pan from the heat and add the mussels to prevent flareups. Reduce heat to medium and cook the mussels for about 30 seconds to 1 minute. Add the garlic, shallots, and chili flakes and cook until fragrant, about 30 seconds.

Deglaze the pan with the white wine and allow the wine to reduce by two-thirds. Once the wine has reduced, add the lobster butter and stir continuously until melted completely and sauce is thickened some. Season with salt and pepper to taste.

To serve: Discard any unopened mussels. Pour mussels and broth into a bowl and serve with warm crusty bread. Garnish with more fresh chives or other herbs, if desired.

* You can make this butter ahead of time and store in the refrigerator or freezer for as long as you want. This recipe also makes 1 pound of butter, which will last for a long time. I use the lobster butter in a bunch of different recipes; it is very versatile.

LETOUR

625 Davis Street, Evanston
(224) 999-7085
letourevanston.com

A James Beard Foundation Award winner and four-time nominee, Chef Debbie Gold took the helm of Amy Morton's restaurants in 2019 after 20 years in Kansas City. It was in Kansas where she earned accolades for her work at The American Restaurant and her own spot, 40 Sardines. Earlier in her career, the Chicago native and three-time contestant on Bravo TV's *Top Chef Masters* worked in some of the most famed restaurants in France and attended Ecole Hoteliere Tain l'Hermitage, an esteemed cooking school in the country. She later continued her training with the legendary Charlie Trotter, holding down every position in the kitchen from hotline to pastry. She then became the pastry chef at Chef Jean Joho's iconic Everest, before accepting the head chef position at Mirador, which was Amy Morton's first venture apart from her late father, famed restaurateur Arnie Morton. Gold says she chose this recipe because "It's like a flavor bomb in your mouth. There are several steps to the dish, but it has a great balance of flavor and textures."

BUTTER BASTED MONKFISH WITH KOHLRABI, BARLEY AND GREEN APPLE
(SERVES 4)

For the monkfish:

2 tablespoons olive oil

2 tablespoons unsalted butter, room temp

4 (6-ounce) fillets monkfish

¼ teaspoon salt, plus more to taste

¼ teaspoon freshly ground black pepper, plus
  more to taste

For the toasted barley risotto:

4 cups vegetable stock

3 tablespoons extra-virgin olive oil

1 cup pearled barley

2 tablespoons unsalted butter

Kosher salt, to taste

For the pickled green apple:

1 granny smith apple, peeled

¼ cup malt, apple cider or beer vinegar

For the kohlrabi:

2 each medium kohlrabi

½ teaspoon kosher salt

For the bonito butter:

2 cups water

2 packets bonito flakes

½ cup white wine

1 cup unsalted butter, room temperature

2 teaspoons lemon juice

To prepare the pickled green apple: Scoop balls
out of the apple using a small Parisian scoop for 12
to 16 balls. Submerge in the vinegar in a medium
bowl or vacuum seal to compress the fruit with the
vinegar. Refrigerate until ready to serve.

To prepare the kohlrabi: Slice or peel the kohlrabi
using a vegetable peeler into very long, thin strips.
Toss with kosher salt and set aside.

To prepare the bonito butter: Bring water to a boil
in a small saucepan. Add bonito flakes and reduce
to ½ cup. Purée mixture in a food processor or using
a hand-held immersion blender. Strain, reserving 1
tablespoon of the pulp. In the same saucepan, bring
the white wine to a simmer and cook until reduced
by half. Take off heat and cool to room temperature.
Add the wine to the food process or, along with the
reserved bonito liquid and pulp, softened butter and
lemon juice. Pulse until smooth. Set aside.

To prepare the barley risotto: Bring the stock to a
boil in a medium saucepan. Reduce heat and maintain a low simmer.

Heat olive oil in a separate, medium saucepan. Add
barley and toast the grains in the oil for 3 to 4 minutes. Add 1 cup of the hot stock to the barley and
cook over medium heat, stirring frequently, until
nearly absorbed. Continue adding broth, ½ cup at a
time, until barley is al dente, about 30 minutes. Stir
in the butter and season with salt. Set aside.

Preheat the oven to 400°F.

To prepare the monkfish: In a large, oven-safe
sauté pan, heat the olive oil and butter until melted.
Season monkfish with salt and pepper. Cook until
golden on both sides, about 2 minutes per side.
Place pan in the oven until fish is cooked through,
about 10 minutes.

To serve: Place a large spoonful of the barley risotto
on the bottom of 4 large bowls. Top with the monkfish fillet. Place kohlrabi ribbons on top of the fish
to form a circle. Drizzle melted bonito butter evenly
over all and garnish with the pickled green apples.

Jeong

1460 W Chicago Avenue
(312) 877-5016
Jeongchicago.com

Chef Dave Park cooks up fine Korean cuisine in the heart of the city's West Town neighborhood, paying homage to his Asian roots. His restaurant's name holds a personal meaning for Park, representing deep emotional attachment in Korean culture. Not only is it his grandmother's maiden name, but it also describes a special type of love that fosters a deep, soulful connection creating a lasting bond between people. This is what he and his wife, Jen Tran, have hoped to convey through their offerings. Park, who was born in Anyang, Korea, found himself immersed in traditional Korean cooking from a young age, cherishing such ingredients as sesame paste and gochujang. At the age of 8, Park moved with his family to New Jersey, spent some time prepping sandwiches at a local family-run restaurant in high school, and decided to attend the Culinary Institute of America in Hyde Park, New York, where he met Tran.

Upon graduating, Park worked in a number of top Chicago institutions, including the Michelin-starred Takashi and The Aviary, where he was part of its opening team under world-renowned chef Grant Achatz. He has also cooked for distinguished United Nations guests. In December 2015, he and Tran opened Hanbun in the Chicago suburbs; the small but formidable stand in a

mall food court instantly earned rave reviews and a cult following. Since opening Jeong in March 2019, he has earned rave reviews from multiple local media outlets. This recipe reflects Park's self-described style as "heartfelt, with childhood flavors refined." One of those childhood flavors for Park is doenjang, a fermented soybean paste found in Asian grocery stores or often in the international section of a traditional grocery store. Note that while gochujang might be more readily available, it is a much spicier product.

SALMON TARTARE WITH DOENJANG AND YUZU CRÈME FRAÎCHE
(SERVES 4)

For the salmon:

1 (roughly 9-ounce) fillet sushi-grade salmon (such as Ora King or Loch Duarte salmon)

For the yuzu doenjang gastrique:

2½ tablespoons Doenjang (37 grams or 1.3 ounces)

1¼ cup water (300 grams or about 10 ounces)

¾ cup sake (150 grams or 5.3 ounces)

¼ cup plus 1 tablespoon yuzu marmalade (70 grams or 2.5 ounces)

For salmon marinade:

1 small shallot, minced (40 grams or 2½ tablespoons)

2 tablespoons yuzu marmalade (30 grams)

3¾ tablespoons white shoyu (55 grams)

2 tablespoons yuzu juice (30 grams)

Zest from 1 lemon

For yuzu whipped crème fraîche:

¾ cup crème fraîche (140 grams)

1 tablespoon (10 grams) yuzu juice

To prepare the salmon: Trim the fillet of excess fat and skin and remove any bones. Slice salmon crosswise into ½-inch-thick pieces. Turn the pieces and slice crosswise into ½-inch pieces. Slice those pieces into ½-inch cubes. Place the diced salmon in a bowl set over another bowl of ice.

To prepare the marinade: Whisk all ingredients together and set aside.

To prepare the gastrique: Combine all ingredients in a small saucepot and bring to a boil. Reduce heat and simmer until thick and syrupy. Blend the mixture in a food processor or blender or using a hand-held immersion blender until smooth. Transfer to the refrigerator to chill.

To prepare the yuzu crème fraîche: Combine the two ingredients in a small bowl, whisking vigorously until medium peaks form. Set aside.

To serve: Working with 1 plate at a time, place about 2 teaspoons of the gastrique in the center of 4 plates.

Set a ring mold or cookie cutter on top of the gastrique. Add the marinade to the bowl with the salmon and toss to combine. Gently press about ½ cup of the salmon tartare in the mold. Gently lift and remove the mold. Garnish with a dollop of the whipped crème fraîche. Repeat with remaining 3 plates.

MI TOCAYA ANTOJERIA

2800 W Logan Boulevard
(872) 315-3947
Mitocaya.com

Self-described as an "antojeria that pays homage to our ances- tors, honors women and our tierra," Chef Diana Dávila's first restaurant does just that. Focused on authentic Mexican dishes with spins here and there, and on local ingredients, the intimate, indoor-outdoor restaurant sits just steps from the site of the Logan Square Farmers Market. A native of the Chicago suburbs, Dávila began working in her parents' taqueria at just 10 years of age. She later cooked at her family's upscale concept, Hacienda Jalapeños, where she received many accolades. Dávila went on to study under Chef Susana Trilling at Season of the Heart culi- nary school in Oaxaca, Mexico, returning to Chicago to work with Chef Ryan Poli at Butter, and later with Chef Giuseppe Tentori as the fish cook for Boka in 2008. After a four-year stint in Washington D.C., she returned to Chicago to open Cantina 1910. When that closed for reasons still undisclosed in 2016, she went on to open the highly acclaimed Mi Tocaya in 2017. Dávila's recipe for esquites, sometimes described as Mexican street corn, takes advantage of the sweet corn harvested in

the summer in the Midwest, elevated by the lobster meat addition. At the restaurant, Dávila has garnished the corn with a lobster-infused crema, queso fresco, lime zest, a chopped epazote and cilantro mix and fried guajillo peppers, but the options are endless. You could also leave out the lobster or swap it with cooked crab meat if more readily available (and affordable).

LOBSTER ESQUITES
(MAKES 3-4 CUPS)

½ cup unsalted butter

1 medium white onion, diced

9 cloves garlic, sliced

1 teaspoon salt

2 cups lobster or chicken stock

3 cups freshly shucked corn kernels (from about 3 or 4 ears)

12 ounces (or 1½ cups) chopped cooked lobster meat

2 serrano peppers, seeded, stemmed, thinly sliced

Crema, crumbled queso fresco, lime zest and wedges, chopped fresh cilantro, chopped epazote, for garnish (optional)

Heat the butter in a large stockpot until melted. Add the onion and garlic and cook until onions are translucent and garlic fragrant, about 2 minutes. Season with salt and cook until mixture resembles a colorless paste, about 3 minutes.

Add corn, peppers and stock. Bring to a boil and cook until liquid has evaporated. Take off heat and add the lobster meat, stirring until warmed through.

Divide esquites between bowls or serve in a large serving bowl or on a platter. Garnish with crema, queso fresco, lime zest and/or lime wedges, chopped fresh cilantro and/or epazote.

THE SIGNATURE ROOM AT THE 95TH

875 N Michigan Avenue
(312) 787-9596
Signatureroom.com

Perched high up in the clouds, The Signature Room on the 95th floor of the formerly named John Hancock building on Chicago's Magnificent Mile has been a beacon for regulars and visitors alike. Chef Cardel Reid, a native whose affinity for food began while cooking alongside his mother growing up, has helmed the kitchen since 2014. He worked many years at the restaurant before that, working up the ranks since beginning as a line cook in 2001. For seven years, he ran the catering department, overseeing many wine dinners and important banquets and cocktail receptions for over 10,000 people at a time. He has also traveled with the restaurant group to cook at the James Beard House and for other notable groups. Prior to taking over as executive chef, Reid spent two years as chef de cuisine under the direction of Chef Patrick Sheerin. This is his easy recipe for a super-comforting dish that can be served alone, as an entrée or starter, or with rice, vegetables or pasta.

SHRIMP DEJONGHE

(SERVES 2)

For the shrimp and garlic butter:

8 large or jumbo tail-on shrimp

1 teaspoon minced garlic

6 tablespoons butter

¼ teaspoon salt, or to taste

⅛ teaspoon freshly ground black pepper, or to taste

For the Parmesan herb breadcrumbs:

2 teaspoons Parmesan cheese

2 teaspoons parsley

2 teaspoons dried thyme

1 tablespoon breadcrumbs

Zest from 1 lemon

To prepare the breadcrumb topping: Heat a small skillet over medium heat. Add all of the ingredients and let sit until toasted, stirring once, about 3 to 4 minutes. Set aside.

To prepare the shrimp and garlic butter: Heat butter in a separate, medium pan over medium heat until melted. Add garlic and cook until browned and fragrant, about 2 minutes. Add shrimp and cook until pink. Season with salt and pepper.

Divide shrimp between two bowls. Pour garlic butter over the shrimp. Sprinkle breadcrumb mixture evenly over all and serve.

Beef, Lamb, and More

Chicago's trademark as a meat-and-potatoes kind of town began with the stockyards and steakhouses that developed post-fire in the 1900s, and later post-World War II.

But since then, and long before investigative writers drew our attention to the way animals are raised and harvested in this country, chefs in Chicago were already building relationships with smaller, non-commercial meat producers in Illinois, Iowa, Indiana and Wisconsin to source not only typical Midwestern hunting game meat but also sustainably produced beef, pork, lamb, and even goat.

Sustainably produced meat means animals are raised on open pastures and/or fed non-GMO grains and, above all, treated with kindness and respect.

CLASSIC CHICAGO STEAKHOUSES

Steakhouses, once considered the fabric of the Chicago restaurant scene, once served as the only type of upscale restaurant open in the city. Shrimp cocktail and oysters on the half shell, giant-size, blood rare and crusty slabs of meat, cheesy twice-baked potatoes, and creamy green spinach—these were and still are the dishes that made these clubby eateries popular during the 1950s and '60s when veterans of the war reentered the workforce with more money to burn and a stronger penchant for cocktailing. Some of the older steakhouses, such as Gene & Georgetti's, once boasted a reservation system as political and tight as a bookie, with celebrities and socialites vying for "the" table to see and be seen. Now, classic steakhouses still abound in Chicago, but many have graduated to a more modern feel, thanks to swanky interiors, wood-fired equipment, inventive cocktails and chef-driven dishes and desserts to start and end the meal.

Prairie Grass Café

601 Skokie Boulevard, Northbrook
(847) 205-4433
Prairiegrasscafe.com

Sarah Stegner and George Bumbaris are a team. During the early 1990s, they raised the Ritz Carlton Dining Room to untold heights. And there, the start of the Slow Food movement in Chicago began; Stegner served as one of the founding board members of Chicago's Green City Market when it opened in 1998. "I believe the food we source locally is always the freshest, and always tastes the best, above everything else," she says. Stegner's also traveled as far as Alaska to trace the source of the halibut she serves, forging lifelong friendships with the family fisheries. At home, she brings in her own family, with pies homemade by her mother. This philosophy, at one point, led to a partnership with TV journalist Bill Kurtis to source his grass-fed, Tallgrass beef. Indeed, the restaurant's name was inspired by the ranch's tall "prairie grass." Today, Prairie Grass enjoys a strong, loyal following, even during the toughest of times.

GRASS-FED BEEF BRISKET WITH PAN-ROASTED PARSNIPS
(SERVES 10-12)

For the brisket:

1 7-8-pound grass-fed beef brisket, such as Tallgrass beef

Kosher salt and freshly ground black pepper, to taste

3 tablespoons olive oil, divided

4 cups diced onion

1 cup peeled and diced carrots

1 cup chopped celery

2 tablespoons minced garlic

1 28-ounce can diced tomatoes, drained

4 bay leaves

4 sprigs fresh thyme

8 cups chicken broth or stock

½ cup packed brown sugar

2 tablespoons unsalted butter

For the parsnips:

10 parsnips, peeled and cut into wedges

2 tablespoons unsalted butter

Kosher salt and freshly ground pepper, to taste

To prepare the brisket: Preheat the oven to 350°F. Season both sides of the meat with salt and pepper. Heat 2 tablespoons of the oil in a large ovenproof sauté pan or roasting pan over medium-high heat and sear brisket to form a crust, about 3-4 minutes per side. Remove from pan.

Add remaining 1 tablespoon oil to the pan and sauté the onions, carrots, and celery until onions are translucent but not browned, about 2-3 minutes. Add the garlic and cook 1 minute more. Stir in the tomatoes and add the bay leaves, thyme, broth, and brown sugar. Bring to a simmer. Return brisket to pan, cover tightly with lid or heavy-duty foil, and roast for 3½-4 hours or until meat is fork tender.

To prepare the parsnips: Blanch parsnips for 3-4 minutes in salted boiling water until tender. Heat butter in a large sauté pan over medium heat. Drain parsnips, add to pan, and sauté until golden brown on all sides and caramelized, about 5-6 minutes.

Remove the brisket from the liquid and set aside to cool slightly. Strain the liquid through a fine-mesh sieve into a medium saucepan, discarding solids. Bring liquid to a boil, turn off heat, and stir in butter.

To serve: Slice the brisket against the grain into ¼-inch-thick pieces and arrange on a platter or in individual ceramic bowls. Pour sauce over brisket and serve alongside pan-roasted parsnips.

BRINDILLE, KOSTALI

534 N Clark Street
(312) 595-1616
Brindille-chicago.com

521 N Rush Street, 5th Floor
(312) 645-1500
Kostalichicago.com

Before the words "local," "sustainable" and "green" took on meanings we know, there was "Carrie." As one of the original board members for Green City Market, Nahabedian, alongside her family, has remained committed to showcasing the best of the Midwest in her dishes at the late Naha, and now at Brindille and Kostali, the latest addition to her restaurant portfolio. Naha was known as the go-to place for fine-dining Mediterranean-inspired cuisine, frequented often by former Chicago Mayor Rahm Emmanuel and other celebrity guests. She hosted a very well-attended "holiday party" at Naha every year where the freshly shucked oysters at the front marble bar and champagne flowed. Along with her cousin Michael (Nahabedian), Nahabedian opened Brindille in 2013 as a more French-inspired outpost that also drew and continues to draw regulars. After Naha closed in 2018 after a strong, 18-year run, the duo teamed up with The Gwen Hotel to open Kostali in the fifth-floor lobby with a menu that draws inspiration from their Armenian and Greek roots.

WALNUT CRUSTED VEAL RIB EYE WITH GRATIN OF CAULIFLOWER, PINK PEPPERCORNS, CONFIT GARLIC, AND SAGE

(SERVES 6)

6 cuts veal rib eye (5-6 oz each)

1 cup walnuts, slightly crushed

½ cup breadcrumbs

2 ounces butter, melted

3 cups cauliflower florets (one head)

8 ounces heavy cream

2 eggs

Fresh thyme sprig

1 tablespoon chopped parsley

1 garlic bulb

2 tablespoons pink peppercorns

16 ounces veal jus (make at home, or buy at a
   specialty store)

1 ounce walnut oil

2 ounces olive oil

Pumpkinseed oil (for serving, optional)

*2 sage sprigs, fresh and fried (optional)

Have a butcher cut 6 pieces of veal rib eye from the veal rack.

Mix the walnuts, breadcrumbs, and melted butter in a bowl. Set aside.

Blanch the cauliflower in salted water. Refresh, and strain. Add heavy cream to a pot and reduce to half on medium heat. Mix the cauliflower, eggs, reduced cream, thyme, parsley, and seasonings to taste. Butter a ceramic mold, fill with the cauliflower mixture and drizzle with the walnut oil. Bake in a preheated oven at 375°F for 20 minutes or until lightly browned.

Peel the garlic cloves and blanch three times in water. On the third blanch, add salt to the water. Pat dry and roast in the oven with olive oil until browned.

Season the veal with salt and cracked black peppercorns. Sear in a heavy sauté pan over medium heat until each side is a rich golden brown. Finish cooking in the oven to the desired temperature – medium to medium-rare takes about 8 minutes. Remove the veal from the pan and deglaze with a splash of white wine and add the veal jus. Over high heat, quickly bring to a boil, lower the flame, and reduce by half. Finish the sauce with a small piece of soft butter, the pink peppercorns, confit garlic and sage. Set aside.

Just before serving, top each piece of veal rib eye with the walnut mixture and flash in the oven.

Spoon the cauliflower gratin onto a plate. Top with the veal, spoon the sauce around the veal and gratin. Drizzle with pumpkinseed oil, top with a crisp fried sage leaf and serve.

*To prepare fried sage leaves:

HOPLEAF

5148 N Clark Street
(773) 334-9851
Hopleafbar.com

When Michael Roper took his first bite of the smoky-cured, pink-colored stack of tender brisket sandwiched between two dark rye bread slices during a trip to Montreal, he knew he wanted to bring the classic combo back to his restaurant in the States. Hopleaf, the Far-North-Side Andersonville institution for craft beer and bistro-inspired comfort food, has been called one of the first "gastropubs" of its kind in Chicago and the country. Chef Ben Sheagren helped him recreate this favorite at the long-running bar and restaurant. The Canadian version, made famous at Schwartz's Deli, differs from U.S. variations in that it's typically herbier, spicier, juicer and meatier. Roper and Sheagren's version uses certified organic beef with a spicy rub of coriander, fennel and cumin stacked high on pumpernickel, but just about any artisan-quality bread will do.

To recreate the traditional pink coloring found in the brisket abroad, use the Insta Cure No. 1, a curing salt mixture, also commonly used for corned beef, available online or in select grocery stores and gourmet retail outlets nationwide.

MONTREAL-STYLE SMOKED BRISKET SANDWICH

(SERVES 8-10)

For the rub:

2 tablespoons whole black peppercorns

½ tablespoon coriander seeds

½ tablespoon cumin seeds

¾ tablespoon fennel seeds

½ tablespoon mustard seeds

1½ tablespoons celery seeds

3 allspice berries

½ tablespoon mustard powder

2 tablespoons smoked paprika

2½ tablespoons light brown sugar

2½ tablespoons kosher salt

2 tablespoons minced garlic

½ teaspoon Insta Cure No. 1 (salt and sodium nitrate) (optional)

For the brisket:

1 5-pound beef brisket

¼-½ pound thick-cut smoked bacon, cut into 6-8 strips

1 cup red wine

¾ cup hickory chips (optional)

To prepare the rub: Preheat oven to 350°F. On a baking sheet arrange peppercorns, coriander, cumin, fennel, mustard seed, celery seed, and allspice berries in a single layer. Toast in the oven for roughly 15-20 minutes, until fragrant and lightly browned. (Alternatively, toast seeds in a large sauté pan, dry, over medium-high heat, stirring often.) Allow to cool to room temperature, then transfer spices to a coffee grinder and grind to a coarse consistency.

In a small bowl, combine the ground spices with the mustard powder, paprika, brown sugar, and salt. Include the Insta Cure No. 1 if a pink meat color is desired.

To prepare the brisket: Rub brisket with the garlic and then with the spice-sugar mixture, working with an aggressive massaging action. Refrigerate meat at least 1-2 hours, up to 48 hours, to allow rub to "marinate" the beef.

Preheat oven or outdoor smoker or grill to 250°F. Place brisket on a roasting pan with a rack. Layer 6-8 slices of thick-cut smoked bacon along the top of the brisket. Add more bacon to completely cover the brisket if not using a smoking process. Pour the red wine in the bottom of pan and slide onto the middle rack of the oven. If you have a smoker option, place enough wet hickory chips in the smoking tray to provide 45 minutes to 1 hour of smoke (approximately 1½ cups), or set the timer on the smoking implement, if available.

Roast or smoke brisket 5 hours, basting with its own juices collected in the pan 3 or 4 times during the final three hours of cooking. The brisket will be done when the meat pulls apart with gentle pressure along the grain (about 180°F internal temperature).

To serve: Allow meat to rest, covered and at room temperature, for half an hour before hand-slicing very thin. Serve with grainy mustard and rye bread or other bread of your choice.

THE PUBLICAN

837 W Fulton Market
(312) 733-9555
Thepublicanrestaurant.com

Revered Chicago chef Paul Kahan and restaurateur Dannie Madia created their third venture, The Publican, in a testament to all things pork, emblemized by the menu of pork chops, belly, hams, ribs and sausages, and by the life-size drawing of a pig on the main wall. At the time when it opened, that was all the rage. While it still is, The Publican today serves many different types of dishes, including many seafood offerings. The duo has arguably built one of the most successful restaurant groups in Chicago. One Off Hospitality's portfolio today includes the long-running avec and new avec River North; Publican Quality Meats (a local butcher and sandwich shop); Publican Quality Bread (a bakery); Big Star; and The Violet Hour, one of Chicago's first upscale cocktail lounges. Sadly, the fine-dining institution, Blackbird, closed in 2020. Sweetbreads—decidedly not an everyday ingredient—can be special ordered from most butchers or purchased online through various companies dedicated to the humane treatment of the animal.

THE PUBLICAN'S VEAL SWEETBREADS
(SERVES 4)

For the court bouillon:

3 quarts cold water

2 750-ml bottles white wine

6 large yellow onions, minced

1 large carrot, sliced

1 rib celery, sliced

Large bouquet garni

½ cup salt

1 tablespoon whole black peppercorns

For the sweetbreads:

1 pound veal sweetbreads, rinsed under cold water

1 cup quick-mixing flour, such as Wondra*

4 tablespoons butter, softened

1 tablespoon palm sugar

2 tablespoons extra-virgin olive oil

To prepare the bouillon: Combine all ingredients for court bouillon in a large saucepan. Bring to a boil over high heat. Reduce heat, add sweetbreads, and poach at a gentle simmer for 5 minutes, stirring once.

Pour sweetbreads and court bouillon into a metal bowl set over a large bowl of ice. Cool sweetbreads, stirring occasionally. Remove sweetbreads; refrigerate court bouillon for another use. Peel off and discard outer membrane from the sweetbreads and separate into four 4-ounce portions. Dredge lightly in flour. Combine butter and palm sugar; set aside.

To prepare the sweetbreads: Sauté the sweetbreads in the oil in a medium skillet until lightly browned on both sides, basting occasionally with the palm sugar butter.

To serve: Serve warm with a variety of sauces (mustard, barbecue, honey, etc.) or treat them as croutons and serve them in a salad.

*Wondra, a flour developed for lump-free blending in sauces and gravies, has lately been used by chefs to create a lighter, airy breading for frying. If Wondra flour is unavailable, combine 1 cup all-purpose flour with 1½ teaspoons baking powder and ½ teaspoon salt. Use this mixture for the recipe.

Beatnik, Porto

1604 W Chicago Avenue
(312) 929-4945
Beatnikchicago.com

180 N Upper Wacker Drive
(312) 526-3345
Beatnikontheriver.com

1600 W Chicago Avenue
(312) 600-6336
Portochicago.com

Chef Marcos Campos, partner/ group executive chef of Bonhomme Hospitality, started cooking in fine-dining restaurants in Spain at the young age of 17. After working in kitchens throughout Europe and Denmark, he came to Chicago and opened a Spanish tapas restaurant called Black Bull with business partner Daniel Alfonso. When Black Bull ran its course, the duo decided to change course and focus on other cuisines from the Middle East, India, North Africa and South America. That became the focus of the menu at Beatnik in the Wicker Park neighborhood. A whimsical design, with plenty of colorful, Moroccan textiles, natural greenery and artful pieces collected during the team's travels throughout the world echo the eclectic nature of the menu. Porto, which opened in 2019, is Campos' return to his roots, with a Spanish and Portuguese seafood menu and handpicked wine list that brings in influences from neighboring Portugal. The wraparound, rectangular bar serves as the focal point for the intimate space as well as an homage to the Spanish tapas style of snacking and sharing meals with one another. Campos' recipe again reflects the eclectic nature of his current cooking style. Though it's meant to be served platter-style, for sharing, you can always divvy up the meatballs into separate plates.

CURRIED MEATBALLS WITH AVOCADO HUMMUS

(SERVES 6-8)

For the meatballs:

2 pounds ground pork

½ pound ground beef

1 tablespoon tomato paste

5 garlic cloves

1 bunch Italian parsley

½ tablespoon curry powder

2 large eggs

1 tablespoon sea or kosher salt

1 teaspoon freshly ground black pepper

High-heat, neutral oil (such as grapeseed, canola, vegetable or avocado) (for frying)

Chopped fresh cilantro, sun-dried tomatoes and/or prepared harissa sauce (optional, for garnish)

Grilled sourdough or crusty bread slices, for serving

For the curry sauce:

⅓ cup neutral oil

8 carrots, chopped

4 yellow or sweet onions, chopped

10 garlic cloves, minced

16 cups chicken stock

5 tablespoons curry powder

For the avocado hummus:

3 avocados

4 cups cooked chickpeas

1 garlic clove

½ bunch cilantro

3 tablespoons lime juice

2 tablespoons extra-virgin olive oil

To prepare the curry sauce: Heat oil in a large saucepan over medium heat. Add the carrots and onions and cook until onions are beginning to brown. Add the garlic and cook until fragrant, about 1 minute. Add stock and curry powder, stirring until combined. Cover and bring to a boil. Reduce to a simmer and cook, uncovered, until vegetables are tender, and half of the liquid has evaporated, about 15 to 20 minutes. Remove from heat and when cool enough to handle, transfer mixture to a blender. Blend until smooth and set aside or cool and refrigerate for later use.

To prepare the avocado hummus: Slice avocados in half and remove pits. Spoon the flesh into the bowl of a food processor. Add the chickpeas, avocado, garlic, cilantro and lime juice. Process until combined and chunky. With the motor running, add the oil and process until very smooth. Set aside or cover and refrigerate for later use.

To prepare the meatballs: Add the tomato paste, herbs, spices and eggs to a large mixing bowl. Mash with a wooden spoon to form a paste. Add the pork and beef, gently mixing to combine. Do not overmix. Refrigerate for at least 1 hour, up to overnight.

Shape the meat into golf ball-size balls. Heat 2 inches of oil in a large skillet over medium heat. When oil is shimmering, working in batches to avoid crowding the pan, add the meatballs, turning occasionally until browned and cooked through in the center, about each batch. Remove meatballs from the oil using a slotted spoon and drain on a paper towel-lined plate or sheet tray.

To serve: Spoon or pour curry sauce onto a serving plate or in a large serving bowl. Top with the meatballs. Serve with the avocado hummus, garnished with cilantro, sun-dried tomatoes and/or a drizzle of harissa, if desired, and crusty, grilled sourdough bread for soaking everything up.

CHEZ MOI

2100 N Halsted Street
(773) 871-2100
Chezmoichicago.com

The late Chef Dominique Tougne opened Chez Moi in 2012 with Cristobal Huet, a former Blackhawks player, after years of 15 serving as the chef de cuisine for Levy Restaurants' Bistro 110. Though Tougne was born in in Alsace, the northeast region of France, he says his family heritage is from Dordogne, in the southwest corner of the country, and Chez Moi's menu reflects this paradigm. At the young the age of fourteen, Tougne began his training at a culinary school in Blois, just outside of Paris. He went on to cook under such French culinary greats as Jacques Senechal and Joel Robuchon. In 2021, in the middle of a global pandemic, Tougne opened French Quiche Chicago, a mostly carryout and catering restaurant offering the experience of a Parisian café, boulangerie and patisserie for the home, complete with freshly baked breads, crepes, quiches and pastries. Here, he offers a recipe for a classic meal intended to serve a hungry crowd.

BRAISED LAMB SHANK MEDITERRANEAN

(SERVES 6-8 [RECIPE CAN BE HALVED FOR A SMALLER PORTION])
COOK TIME: 4-5 HOURS

6 each lamb fore shanks

Sea salt

1 tablespoon neutral, high-heat oil (such as
    grapeseed, avocado or canola)

2 teaspoons cumin

2 teaspoons coriander

1 teaspoon curry powder

¼ teaspoon freshly ground black pepper, to taste

1 large onion, diced

1 large carrot, diced

5 garlic cloves, chopped

2 sprigs fresh thyme, plus extra leaves for garnish

1 sprig rosemary, plus extra leaves for garnish

2 bay leaves

Chicken stock

4 teaspoons olive oil

Cooked mashed potatoes, couscous or white beans
    (for serving)

Preheat the oven to 320°F.

Season lamb shanks liberally with salt. Heat oil in a large Dutch oven or deep cast iron over medium-high heat. Add lamb shanks and sear until browned on both sides, flipping once, about 5 to 7 minutes. Turn off heat and transfer shanks to a sheet pan and allow to cool slightly.

Combine the cumin, coriander, curry powder and pepper in a small bowl. When spice mixture is cool enough to handle, rub shanks with it, massaging for up to 2 minutes to work in the spices.

Reheat the Dutch oven over medium heat. Add onions and carrots and cook until onions are soft and translucent, about 2 minutes. Add garlic and cook until fragrant, 1 minute. Add thyme, rosemary, bay leaves, reserved lamb shanks and enough chicken stock to cover. Cover and bring to a boil.

Turn off heat and remove lid. Cover loosely with foil and transfer to the oven. A loose cover will allow excess liquid to evaporate for the sauce.

Braise shanks until meat is tender, turning once, and liquid has reduced a bit, about 3 hours.

Remove shanks and set aside on a sheet tray. Remove and discard thyme and rosemary stems and bay leaves. Use a hand mixer or handheld immersion blender or transfer liquid and vegetables to a blender and blend until smooth.

Turn up oven heat to broil. Drizzle olive oil over lamb shanks and transfer sheet tray with the shanks to the oven. Broil until a crust develops on the surface, about 2 to 3 minutes.

Serve shanks with mashed potatoes, couscous or white beans and top with the sauce. Garnish with reserved rosemary and thyme leaves.

EL CHE STEAKHOUSE & BAR

845 W Washington Boulevard
(312) 265-1130
Elchechicago.com

"Chicago always been known for warmth and hospitality," says Chef John Manion, who made his name with the popular La Sirena Clandestina, the West Loop fixture inspired by Manion's time spent in Argentina as a child and later as a cook and budding chef. La Sirena closed after a five-year run when a lease agreement ran out, at which point Manion opened El Che Steakhouse, an extension of the Argentine-style grilled meats offered at his first restaurant, with plenty of live-fire, barbecued steaks and empanadas. During the global pandemic of 2020, Manion created a pop-up butcher shop to continue serving customers and keep up business while dine-in remained closed. That venture morphed into a permanent business, El Che Meat + Provisions, which offers various cuts of raw steaks for grilling at home, as well as other staples like Manion's famous chimichurri recipe (next page), which he says you can prepare using a food processor to cut down on chopping time. Though Manion suggests tying the beef tenderloin, he says most butchers "worth their salt" will tie a whole tenderloin for you.

BEEF TENDERLOIN WITH CHIMICHURRI
(SERVES 2-4)

For the chimichurri

3 cups flat-leaf parsley leaves (from about 3 bunches), finely chopped

6 garlic cloves, finely chopped

1½ teaspoons finely chopped fresh oregano leaves or 1 teaspoon dried oregano

¼ cup distilled white vinegar

1 teaspoon kosher salt

1 teaspoon freshly ground black pepper

1 bay leaf

¾ teaspoon dried red pepper flakes

¾ cup extra-virgin olive oil

For the beef tenderloin:

1 whole beef tenderloin, trimmed of silver skin and tied into a roast

Salt and freshly ground black pepper

Extra-virgin olive oil

To prepare the chimichurri: In a medium-size airtight container, stir together the parsley, garlic, oregano, vinegar, salt, pepper, bay leaf and red pepper flakes.

Stir in the olive oil, cover and refrigerate the chimichurri sauce for at least a few hours, or overnight. Chimichurri will last in the refrigerator for 2 weeks; remove from the fridge at least 30 minutes in advance of serving to bring oil to room temperature (it's normal for the oil to congeal in colder temperatures).

To prepare the beef tenderloin: Preheat the oven to 475°F.

Place tenderloin on a roasting rack and liberally season with salt and pepper. Drizzle a light layer of olive oil over the tenderloin, massaging to rub in the seasoning.

Roast the tenderloin for 20 to 25 minutes, or until internal temperature reaches 120°F to 125°F for medium-rare (temperature will continue to rise 5 to 10 degrees while resting). Remove tenderloin from the oven and set aside. Spoon enough chimichurri over the tenderloin to cover. Let rest, covered loosely with aluminum foil, for about 10 minutes.

Slice against the grain into 1½-inch-thick pieces and serve with extra chimichurri.

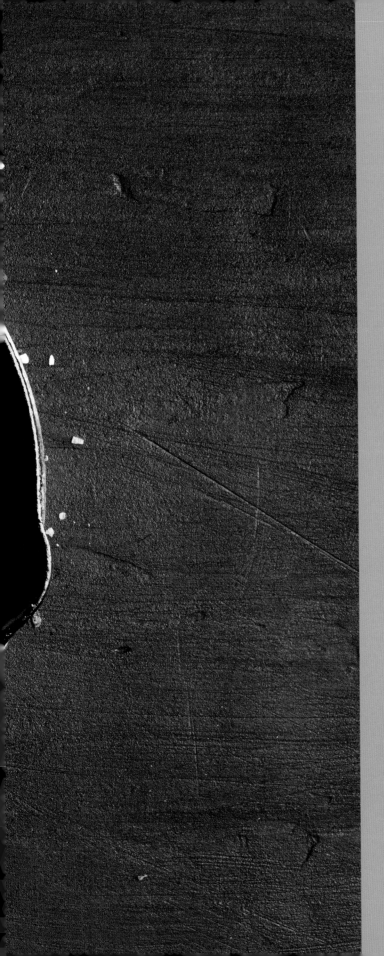

Pork

Once declared the largest hog producer in the nation, Illinois falls far short of Iowa in pork production, but it thrives on family-farm, noncommercial production the best of artisan meats. What does artisan mean? Until only recently, the everyday consumer couldn't access the thick-cut, fatty and juicy cuts of Berkshire pork commonly snatched up by high-end restaurants in New York, and later in Chicago. Now, more butchers and even grocery stores large and small are offering more sustainable pork options, with pigs grown outdoors on pasture—even fed acorns in some cases. Chicago chefs went hog-crazy in the mid-2000s with access to this fattier, delicious meat, even causing pork-centric restaurants like Purple Pig and The Publican to spring up in dedication of the animal. There's even an annual Baconfest held here and around the nation—a celebration of the pig with top chefs from all over the country. While the pork trend has slowed a bit with more plant-based eating on the rise, it's still a much sought-after treat—an ongoing testament to Chicago's Midwestern-meat culture.

avec/avec River North

avec
615 W. Randolph Street
(312) 377-2002

avec River North/bar avec
141 W. Erie Street
(312) 736-1778
Avecrestaurant.com

Considered by many as the birthplace of "small plates," Paul Kahan's avec has been a mainstay in Chicago since 2003. Still situated in the same spot next to Kahan's former fine-dining restaurant Blackbird on Randolph Street (aka, Restaurant Row), avec has seen the rise of many successful chefs and was most recently helmed by Chef Perry Hendrix, whose culinary career has taken him from Asheville, North Carolina, to Salt Lake City, St. Louis, and Chicago in 2013, when he took over as chef of avec in West Loop. Hendrix has since been promoted to One Off Hospitality's culinary creative director in 2020, passing the chef de cuisine title of avec to Chef Dylan Patel, a Chicago native and graduate of the local Kendall College. Both Hendrix and Patel were part of the One Off team that in 2021 helped reconcept the former Pacific Standard Time in River North as a larger secondary location at 5,000 square feet for the ever-popular avec—originally conceptualized as a wine bar and that still retains that intimate feel. Patel also oversees bar avec, avec River North's accompanying eighth-floor rooftop restaurant. The following is a recipe for one of avec's signature small plates that has stood the test of time. If jarred piquillo peppers are difficult to find, substitute roasted red peppers, and make sure to buy uncured, fresh chorizo sausage for the recipe, not the salami-like cured kind.

CHORIZO-STUFFED BACON-WRAPPED DATES

MAKES 8 SERVINGS

1 tablespoon extra-virgin olive oil

8 cloves garlic, thinly sliced

8 small shallots, thinly sliced

8 ounces (about 1 cup) roasted piquillo peppers
with any jar juices, or any roasted red peppers
plus juices

2 cups whole peeled canned tomatoes

kosher salt

freshly ground black pepper

16 Medjool dates, pitted

8 ounces fresh (uncured) chorizo sausage,
casings removed

8 slices bacon

To make the sauce: Heat the oil in a large sauce-pan over medium heat. Add the garlic and shallots and cook until tender, about 5 minutes. Add the peppers and tomatoes, reduce the heat to low, and cook for 30 minutes to 1 hour, until the liquid in the sauce has mostly evaporated. Season with salt and pepper.

Let the sauce cool slightly, then transfer it to a blender and blend until smooth. Thin with warm water, if necessary. You want it to be thick but not so thick that it mounds on the plate.

To make the dates: Preheat the oven to 350°F. Stuff the dates with the chorizo, using about 1½ teaspoons of chorizo per date. Cut the bacon slices in half lengthwise and wrap a slice around each date. Arrange the dates on a small baking sheet and bake for 15 minutes, or until the chorizo is cooked through. Preheat the broiler. Broil the dates for 2 to 4 minutes, until the bacon is dark brown and crisp.

To serve: Spread the sauce over a serving plate and place the dates over the top. Serve warm.

THE PURPLE PIG

500 North Michigan Avenue, Mag Mile
(312) 464-1744
Thepurplepigchicago.com

Chef Jimmy Bannos, Jr., son of the acclaimed Heaven on Seven owner Jimmy Bannos, has led The Purple Pig to be one of the top dining destinations in downtown Chicago, flocked to by locals and visitors alike, thanks in part to its location right on Michigan Avenue. "We focus on nose-to-tail cooking, as they call it," Bannos Jr., says. "We experiment with a lot of different ingredients, like pig's ears, liver and tail, but keep it all approachable and simple." Bannos Jr. at one point even accomplished the impossible: making pigs' ears one of the best=-selling dishes on the menu. "Pork is important to so many cuisines, from Italy to Spain and other Mediterranean cuisines," says Bannos Jr., who earned the top title as "Best Chef: Great Lakes" from the James Beard Award foundation in 2014. A fourth-generation restaurateur, born and raised in Chicago, he was put to work bussing tables for his father at age five, later going on to graduate from Johnson & Wales University. He has also worked at the critically acclaimed Al Forno restaurant and completed an internship with mentor and friend, Chef Emeril Lagasse, earlier in his career.

MILK-BRAISED PORK SHOULDER AND CREAMY MASHED POTATOES

(SERVES 8)

For the pork:

3-4 pounds pork shoulder, bone removed, cut into 8-ounce pieces

Salt and freshly ground black pepper, to taste

2 tablespoons canola or grapeseed oil

4 onions, peeled and quartered

4 large carrots, peeled and cut into large pieces

2 celery ribs, cut into 6 pieces

1 small bunch fresh thyme

5 bay leaves

2 gallons milk

2 gallons pork stock, chicken stock, or low sodium chicken broth

For the potatoes:

1¼ pound russet potatoes, peeled and cut into 1½-inch chunks

¼ cup heavy cream

4 teaspoons butter

½ teaspoon salt

¼ teaspoon freshly ground black pepper

To prepare the pork: Preheat oven to 350°F.

Season pork with salt and pepper. Wrap a piece of string around each pork piece from one end to the other, securing tightly like a small roast.

In a large roasting pan over medium-high heat, using two burners, heat oil and sear pork to create a caramelized crust and hold in juices, about 2-3 minutes per side. Add vegetables, herbs, milk, and stock and bring to a boil.

Slide roasting pan into the oven and roast until pork and vegetables are tender, 2-3 hours.

To prepare the mashed potatoes: Cover potatoes in a large stockpot with salted water. Bring to a boil and cook until tender, 15-20 minutes. While they are cooking, warm the cream. Drain potatoes and return to the pot. Mash using a potato masher or wooden spoon; add cream, butter, salt, and pepper and continue mashing until well mixed. Set aside.

Drain pork and vegetables, reserving 2 cups of the liquid. Chop vegetables into small pieces and set aside. Remove string from pork and slice against the grain into 2-inch-thick slices.

In a small saucepan, reduce liquid to about half or until it thickens slightly. Scoop mashed potatoes onto eight plates, top with vegetables and pork slices, and drizzle with sauce.

Big Star

1531 N Damen Avenue
(773) 235-4039
Bigstarchicago.com

Chef Justin Large developed this recipe for the now top selling taco at Big Star, when he served as chef de cuisine there and also as Chef Paul Kahan's second-in-command (director of culinary operations) for many years, helping open One Off Hospitality Group's many restaurants, which have garnered many awards and accolades. A graduate of the prestigious Culinary Institute of America in Hyde Park, New York, Large has also had multiple appearances on Food Network's Iron Chef and other shows, and he is a founding member of Pilot Light (along with Chef Jason Hammel, p. 51), a non-profit that provides Chicago public schools with skills for healthier eating. Large later went on to briefly serve as executive chef at Guildhall in the northern Chicago suburb of Glencoe. Still, his tacos al pastor are a favorite far and wide. Legend has it that tacos al pastor developed in Mexico when Lebanese immigrants introduced the locals to shawarma, or spit-grilled meat, usually made with lamb. In Mexico, where lamb is scarcer, the tacos are typically made with pork. The pork is marinated overnight or for two days in a liquid chile mixture, rubbed with spices, and then roasted on a spit or vertical rotisserie. Basting with pineapple juice helps tenderize and caramelize the meat further. This is the recipe for a just as flavorful, at-home version.

TACOS AL PASTOR (SPIT-ROASTED PORK TACOS)
(SERVES 6-12)

For the marinade:

2 ounces guajillo chiles

½ ounce ancho chiles

½ tablespoon canned chipotle chiles, drained and finely chopped

¼ cup orange juice

Dash of cocktail bitters

2 ounces Coca-Cola

¼ cup plus 2 tablespoons apple cider vinegar

1 tablespoon light brown sugar

½ clove garlic, minced

For the spice rub:

1½ teaspoons annatto seed

¾ teaspoon dried oregano

¼ teaspoon cumin seed

¼ teaspoon ground cinnamon

2 whole cloves

½ teaspoon whole black peppercorns

1 teaspoon salt

1 teaspoon brown sugar

2 whole garlic cloves

For the pork:

2 pounds boneless pork shoulder or pork butt roast

2 small yellow onions, quartered

¼ fresh pineapple, cut into thick slices

½ dried chile de arbol pepper, minced

½ cup pineapple juice

For serving:

Corn tortillas

1 small red onion, diced

1 bunch cilantro, chopped

To prepare the marinade: Stem and seed the guajillo and ancho chiles, breaking each into small pieces. Soak the chiles in boiling water for 30 minutes. Drain the chiles and place in a blender. Add orange juice, bitters, Coca-Cola, and vinegar and pulse until smooth. Add the sugar and garlic and blend an additional 30 seconds. Pour marinade over pork in a large plastic resealable bag or large bowl. Close bag or cover bowl. Refrigerate pork at least 6–8 hours or overnight, but no more than 36 hours, turning pork over once.

To prepare the spice rub: Preheat oven to 350°F. Discard marinade and lightly pat pork dry with paper towels. Grind the annatto seed, oregano, cumin, cinnamon, cloves, and peppercorns together in a grinder or crush using a mortar and pestle. Combine spices with the salt, sugar, and garlic and rub spice mixture on all sides of pork.

To prepare the pork: Place pork in a shallow roasting pan with the onion. Line pineapple slices along the top of the pork. Make a basting sauce by stirring the chile de arbol into the pineapple juice. Bake 3 hours or until pork is very tender, basting the pork with the juice mixture several times.

Remove pork from oven and let rest 10 minutes. Thinly slice pork or use two forks to pull the pork into shreds.

To serve: Serve with the roasted onion and pineapple on warmed corn tortillas garnished with the red onion and cilantro.

SWIFT & SONS

1000 W Fulton Market
(312) 733-9420
Swiftandsonschicago.com

Since opening The Bristol in 2008, Chef Chris Pandel has become known for some of Chicago's most beloved neighborhood restaurants, where he was one of the early adopters of supporting local farms and for his "nose-to-tail" approach to cooking. In 2012, Pandel and Boka Restaurant Group opened Balena, an ode to Italian-inspired simplicity in Chicago's Lincoln Park. It was here that Pandel became known also for his handmade pasta, wood-fired pizzas and farm-fresh meat dishes. After earning many accolades in that post, in 2015, along with Boka Restaurant Group and B. Hospitality Co., Pandel opened Swift & Sons, a retro-modern steakhouse that celebrates the history of Chicago's meatpacking district. In December 2015, Pandel also opened Cold Storage, located adjacent to Swift & Sons, which is now part of the main restaurant. The oyster bar boasts a daily rotating raw bar along with other seafood-focused salads and sandwiches. With the development of The Hoxton, Chicago in 2019, Pandel opened Cira—an all-day restaurant celebrating Mediterranean flavors. Building on the success of Swift & Sons steakhouse, Pandel oversaw the expansion of the Swift & Sons "brand," with Swift & Sons Tavern combining the steakhouse and oyster bar concepts in the heart of Wrigleyville, directly across from the Chicago Cubs' Wrigley Field. He developed this recipe as a spin on the classic Italian dish, vitello tonnato, typically made with veal and a creamy tuna sauce while at The Bristol, but it still holds popular today.

BACON-WRAPPED PORK LOIN TONNATO
(SERVES 6-8)

For the pork and brine:

2 cups kosher salt

1 tablespoon curing salt, optional

1 cup sugar

4 quarts water

2 cloves garlic, minced

10 whole black peppercorns

5 sprigs fresh rosemary

10 parsley stems

1 bay leaf

1 boneless pork loin, about 4½ pounds

12–14 slices (about 1 pound) thick-cut bacon

For the garlic aioli:

4 egg yolks

1 clove fresh garlic, finely grated

Dash of white or rice vinegar

Pinch of salt

2 cups vegetable oil

For the tonnato sauce:

1 3-ounce can Albacore tuna packed in oil, drained

3 tablespoons minced capers

3 tablespoons minced red onion

½ teaspoon minced fresh marjoram

¼ cup thinly sliced fresh parsley leaves

1 tablespoon red wine vinegar

1 oil-packed anchovy fillet, mashed

Juice of ½ lemon

¼ teaspoon kosher salt

¼ teaspoon freshly ground black pepper

For the salad:

6 tablespoons extra-virgin olive oil

2 tablespoons freshly squeezed lemon juice

Pinch of kosher salt and freshly ground black
    pepper

2 bunches fresh arugula (about ½ pound)

2 tablespoons (½ ounce) shaved Pecorino

Romano cheese

To prepare the brine: In a large bowl, stir together salt, curing salt (if desired) sugar, and water until dissolved. Add garlic, peppercorns, and herbs and pour over pork loin in a deep roasting pan or Cambro cooler. Brine pork in refrigerator for at least 4 hours or up to three days before roasting.

Preheat oven to 300°F.

Discard brine and pat pork loin dry. Wrap the bacon slices around the pork loin to cover completely, tying with string to secure. Roast pork until internal temperature reads 145°F, checking after 30 minutes. When done, let rest 10 minutes. Refrigerate at least 1 hour or overnight.

To prepare the garlic aioli: In a food processor or blender, place the yolks, garlic, vinegar, and salt, pulsing a few times to combine. Blending at moderate speed, slowly pour in the vegetable oil until mixture becomes thick and creamy. Alternatively, whisk together the first four ingredients by hand in a large bowl and slowly pour in the oil, whisking constantly.

To prepare the tonnato sauce: Add the tuna to the aioli in the food processor or blender, and process until smooth. If mixing by hand, mash tuna thoroughly before incorporating into aioli. Scrape tuna mixture into a bowl. Fold in remaining ingredients and adjust seasonings as necessary.

To serve: Slice pork loin into thin pieces and arrange on six or eight plates. Drizzle tonnato sauce evenly over pork. Whisk together oil, lemon juice, salt, and pepper and toss with arugula to coat. Arrange salad evenly atop pork. Garnish with Pecorino shavings.

URBaN BeLLY

1542 N Damen Avenue
(773) 904-8606
Urbanbellychicago.com

Chef Bill Kim has become a household name in Chicago,
thanks to his long-running Urbanbelly restaurant that
was one of the first to introduce a wider group of Chicagoans to various twists on ramen and other brothy noodle
bowls. Urbanbelly moved from its smaller, no-reservations
Andersonville digs to a larger space at the west end of
Randolph Street, becoming one of the first hot restaurants
to populate what is now dubbed Chicago's "Restaurant
Row." That morphed into BellyQ, an upscale Korean
barbecue restaurant with Urbanbelly taking shape as a
smaller, carry-out side within the same space (Urbanbelly later moved to take over Belly Shack, another Kim
concept in Wicker Park). In 2018, Kim and Cornerstone
Restaurant Group (which previously ran Michael Jordan's

One Sixtyblue in the same building) closed BellyQ, but Urbanbelly remains open at the Wicker Park spot. Kim has also partnered with Crate & Barrel to oversee the menu and kitchen at the retail giant's onsite restaurant, The Table at Crate, in Oak Brook, where Kim has shifted gears a bit and offers more vegetable-forward, lighter offerings reflective of how he and his wife prefer to eat these days. His signature kimchi stew recipe is a throwback to the early days when it could easily be said Kim made pork belly famous. For a good while, it was the hot item on menus across town. Thankfully, it's easier today to source pork belly; a special order is sometimes required, but it's worth the effort.

KIMCHI STEW WITH BRAISED PORK BELLY
(SERVES 6)

For the pork:

1 cup fish sauce

½ cup sweet chile sauce

½ cup brown sugar

½ cup mirin

½ cup Sriracha

½ cup Korean chile paste

4 pounds of pork belly or pork butt, cut in pieces to fit in roasting pan

For the broth:

6 cups unsalted or low-sodium chicken stock or broth

2½ cups sweet chile sauce

1 cup soy sauce

1 cup fish sauce

½ cup Korean chile paste

2 pounds flat, oval Korean rice cakes

2 cups chopped napa kimchi

1 12-ounce can hominy, rinsed

Juice of 2 limes

For the garnish:

2 tablespoons toasted cumin seeds

¼ cup chopped cilantro

¼ cup chopped garlic chives

Preheat the oven to 300°F.

To prepare the pork: Combine the fish sauce, sweet chile sauce, brown sugar, mirin, Sriracha, and chile paste in a large bowl. Pour mixture over the pork until almost completely covered.

Roast pork in the oven for about 2 hours, turning after 1 hour. The pork should be tender and cooked through. Remove from oven. When cool enough to handle, cut pork into 1-inch chunks and set aside.

To prepare the broth: Heat chicken broth in a large pot over medium-high heat. Add the sweet chile sauce, soy sauce, fish sauce, and Korean chile paste and simmer for 5 minutes. Add the pork, rice cakes, napa kimchi, and hominy and continue to simmer until rice cakes are tender, about 5 more minutes.

Add lime juice and ladle stew evenly into 6 bowls. Garnish with toasted cumin, chopped cilantro, and garlic chives.

arun's

4156 North Kedzie Avenue, Irving Park
(773) 539-1909
Arunsthai.com

Where Joho has fine-dining French, Mantuano has fine-dining Italian, Bayless has fine-dining Mexican, and Trotter has fine-dining American, Arun Sampanthavivat has fine-dining Thai. Since 1985, the restaurant has also claimed national status as one of the first places to introduce Americans to this authentic, upscale version of Thai cuisine, far from the Americanized pad thai and peanut-sauce-drenched dishes prevalent throughout the city and country.

Originally opening in a tiny six-table storefront, Sampanthavivat relocated down the street a couple years later to a larger but still relatively intimate space. He's also helped elevate the once barren Albany Park neighborhood, which has seen a burgeoning Thai population over the years. Sampanthavivat has teamed with local aldermen, architects, city planners, and investors to help redevelop the area, including rehabbing the former district police station for the Thai Town Center, a community center that will house a spa and wellness center, educational and cultural space, and Sampanthavivat's second restaurant and retail outlet, plus a public-access rooftop garden.

Here Sampanthavivat shares his recipe for hung lay curry, one of northern Thailand's most important curry dishes, he says, which is eaten both as a daily meal and on all festive occasions.

With plenty of ginger and turmeric, the dish represents a classic Burmese-style curry, yet brightened by fresh herbs and lemongrass. Choose a skinless pork belly—five-layer pork, the Chinese call it. Then, Sampanthavivat says, take your time. Slow cooking this curry will result in a much richer flavor and tender pork that melts like butter.

HUNG LAY CURRY (TURMERIC-MARINATED PORK CURRY)
(SERVES 8-10)

For the pork, the marinade, and the chile paste:

3 pounds lean, skinless pork belly, cut into 3-inch squares

½ cup plus 2 tablespoons corn oil, divided

½ teaspoon sweet soy sauce

1½ teaspoons salt, divided

2 tablespoons chopped cilantro leaves, divided

2 tablespoons minced fresh ginger root, divided

¼ cup minced fresh turmeric root, divided

15 garlic cloves, minced, divided

3 shallots, minced, divided

10 dried guajillo chile peppers, soaked in warm water for 30 minutes, drained

10 dried chile de arbol peppers, stems removed

For the stir-fry:

1 teaspoon curry powder or hung lay spices

1 teaspoon fish paste

1–2 cups cold water or chicken stock, as needed

¾ cup palm sugar

3–4 teaspoons fish sauce

1 teaspoon paprika

1 cup tamarind juice

2 lemongrass stalks, white part only, crushed

6–7 kaffir lime leaves (bai makrude), torn into pieces

To prepare the pork belly: Marinate the pork belly. In a resealable plastic bag or a bowl, combine pork with ½ cup oil, ½ teaspoon soy sauce, 1 teaspoon salt, 1 tablespoon cilantro, and half each of the ginger, turmeric, garlic, and shallots. Cover and refrigerate for at least 1 hour.

To prepare the chile paste: In a blender or food processor, add the guajillo and chile de arbol peppers, the remaining ½ teaspoon salt, and the remaining turmeric, garlic, shallot, and cilantro. Blend until smooth. Alternatively, pound ingredients to a paste in a mortar and pestle. Set aside.

To prepare the stir-fry: Heat remaining 2 tablespoons oil in a large skillet over medium-high heat. Drain pork, discarding marinade. Toss pork with the chile paste, curry powder, and fish paste, tossing to combine. Partially cook the pork, tossing occasionally, about 5 minutes or until slightly firm to the touch. Add water or chicken stock, 1 tablespoon at a time, as necessary to prevent scorching.

Add palm sugar, fish sauce, paprika, tamarind juice, and lemongrass. Cover and simmer over medium-low heat until pork is fork tender, about 2–3 hours. Pour in enough stock or water to cover pork, if needed.

To serve: Divide curry into 8–10 bowls. Top with lime leaves and remaining freshly minced ginger. Serve with jasmine rice or sticky rice.

café Ba-Ba-ReeBa!

2024 N Halsted Street
(773) 935-5000
Cafebabareeba.com

Originally from Oak Park, Chef Eric Jorgensen graduated from Chicago's Kendall College with a B.A. in culinary management, going on to serve as executive sous chef at SushiSamba in Chicago before transferring to the New York City locations. At SushiSamba, Jorgensen executed a diverse menu celebrating the cuisine of Japan, Brazil and Peru, which allowed him to develop his own cooking style of incorporating ingredients from different cultures into his dishes. In 2011, Jorgensen moved on to The Mermaid Oyster Bar in New York where he was the chef de cuisine, responsible for creating seasonal menus highlighting sustainable seafood. He moved back to Chicago and signed on with the Lettuce Entertain You Enterprises in 2014 as sous chef at the long-running, ever-popular Cafe Ba-Ba-Reeba! in Lincoln Park. After a short stint in the fast-casual sector, he returned to Cafe Ba-Ba-Reeba! as executive chef in 2017. Lil' Ba-Ba-Reeba, a smaller sister outpost in River North, opened in early 2021.

Jorgensen is a big fan of paella as the perfect party dish because it's a one-pan meal that finishes in the oven without the need to slave over a stove. In order to achieve the socarrat, or the crispy rice crust that forms on the bottom that is a prized part of any properly made paella, you are going to need a carbon steel paella pan," he says, making an exception to his avoidance of single-use kitchen staples. "They are thin and wide to allow as much rice as possible to have contact with the pan. The shape helps with heat distribution and evaporation to make sure your rice is fluffy, not soggy." Jorgensen recommends choosing rice that is rounded and short but stays firm during the cooking process and absorbs liquid well—this includes Bomba or Calasparra rice, but he says Arborio is also an acceptable substitute, just avoid long-grain rice. "When done, the rice should have separate grains glistening with oil and flavor; it shouldn't be creamy or mushy like risotto," he says, suggesting to lightly toast the saffron threads in a 350°F oven or toaster oven for about 10 seconds to bring out flavor and dry out to make it easier to crush with a spoon into a powder.

PAELLA MIXTA
(SERVES 2-4)

4 tablespoons extra-virgin olive oil

½ cup salchichón (spicy, dry-cured Spanish sausage) or Spanish chorizo, diced

½ cup boneless skinless chicken thighs, cubed

½ cup pork shoulder, cubed

1 garlic clove, minced

1 teaspoon paprika

3 ounces tomato purée or canned tomato sauce

1 cup Bomba (paella) rice

2 threads saffron, crushed

½ cup snap peas, halved

1 cup chicken stock

1 cup fish stock (or 1 extra cup chicken stock or 1 cup clam juice)

¼ teaspoon salt, plus more if needed

Chopped fresh parsley leaves, for garnish (optional)

Preheat the oven to 450°F.

Heat the oil in a paella pan or large skillet over medium-high heat. Add the pork and chicken and sear until golden brown, stirring occasionally, about 8 minutes.

Add salchichón, garlic, paprika and tomato purée, stirring to combine. Add the rice, stirring well to coat so that the rice absorbs the olive oil and is sealed before adding the liquid (this prevents the rice from releasing its starch and keeps it firm). Add saffron and stir until fragrant, about 1 minute.

Add the snap peas and stocks, stirring constantly until the rice begins to float. Season with salt and bring to a boil.

Transfer pan to the oven and bake until meat is cooked through and rice is al dente, about 17 minutes. Remove from the oven and let rest for 2 minutes so that the rice absorbs the liquid completely.

Spoon paella into bowls, garnish with parsley, if desired, and serve immediately.

FUNKENHAUSEN

1709 W Chicago Avenue
(312) 929-4727
Funkenhausen.com

Chef Mark Steuer made a name for himself in Chicago while at The Bedford, a sceney restaurant and bar housed in an historic, former bank building in Wicker Park. His first experience in the kitchen began in Charleston, where he grew up and worked with restaurateur Brett McKee. After moving to Chicago in 2006, he got a job working with Mindy Segal at the then Mindy's Hot Chocolate. Other positions followed at Rootstock and The Gage before conceptualizing and creating Carriage House, which focused on low country fare. Now, as chef/owner of Funkenhausen since 2018, Steuer continues his love of pork and seafood with "a culmination of all of my cooking styles throughout the years," says Steuer, who grew up on traditional German food as the son of German immigrants. This is reflected in the restaurant's heavily German menu with Southern influences in a mashup of Bavarian and more low country cuisine. For his stepped-up pork chops, Steuer sources dry-aged pork chops from local Slagel Family Farm, but he says any high-quality pork chop will do. "We brine them overnight, then cook them to order on our wood burning grill," he says, noting that a good charcoal or even gas home grill will work just as well for the home cook.

PORK CHOPS WITH BOURBON SAUCE, CARROT PUREE AND SPICY PEPPER JELLY

(SERVES 4)

For the pork chops and vegetables:

4 (8- to 10-ounce) bone-in pork chops

Salt

Freshly ground black pepper

For the brine:

1 yellow onion, chopped

3 garlic cloves, chopped

1 tablespoons olive oil

4 tablespoons chopped rosemary leaves

4 tablespoons chopped fresh parsley

2 tablespoons dried thyme

1 tablespoon mustard seeds

1 tablespoon fennel seeds

½ tablespoon red chili flakes

½ tablespoons freshly ground black pepper

1 cup kosher salt

1 cup sugar

½ cup apple cider vinegar

1 gallon water, to cover

For the bourbon sauce:

2 tablespoons olive oil

2 white onions

8 cloves garlic

4 tablespoons tomato paste

1 quart bourbon

1 cup red wine

½ cup Worcestershire

1 cup red wine vinegar

8 quarts beef or veal stock

Salt and pepper, to taste

½ can black truffle peelings (optional)

1 cup whole grain mustard

2 tablespoons fresh thyme leaves

For the carrot puree:

1 pound carrots, peeled and diced

1 cloves garlic

½ teaspoon coriander seeds

¼ teaspoon salt

¼ tablespoon lemon juice

¼ cup neutral or blended olive oil and neutral oil

For the spicy pepper jelly:

2 red bell peppers

2 Fresno peppers, stemmed, seeded, roughly chopped

1 jalapeno pepper, stemmed, seeded, roughly chopped

¼ white vinegar

¼ cup cider vinegar

½ teaspoon Old Bay Seasoning

3 cups sugar

4 sheets gelatin, bloomed

¼ teaspoons crushed red pepper flakes, plus more to taste

To prepare the brine: Heat oil in a large saucepot over medium heat. Add the onions and garlic and cook until softened and fragrant, about 2 minutes. Add the herbs, spices, salt, sugar, vinegar and water. Bring to a boil and immediately turn off heat.

Pour brine into a container and chill in an ice bath. Add pork chops to the brine and refrigerate for at least 6 hours to overnight.

Remove pork chops from the brine and pat dry. Season liberally with salt and pepper. Set aside to allow to come to room temperature while preparing the sides.

To prepare the bourbon sauce: Heat oil in a medium saucepan over medium heat. Add the onions and cook until soft and translucent, about 2 minutes. Add the garlic and cook until fragrant, 1 minute. Push aside onions and garlic and add tomato paste to the center of the pan. Let sit to caramelize, 1 minute. Stir to combine.

Add the bourbon and wine and cook until alcohol is burned off, about 2 minutes. Add the Worcestershire, vinegar, stock and, if using, truffles. Bring to a simmer and reduce by half. Transfer sauce to a blender and process until smooth. Stir in mustard and thyme and set aside.

To prepare the carrot purée: Combine the carrots, garlic and coriander seeds in a large saucepot and cover with water. Season with salt and bring to a simmer. Cook until carrots are tender, about 10 to 15 minutes. Strain carrots, reserving the liquid, into a blender or food process. Add lemon juice and with the motor running, slowly add oil until creamy and smooth. Set aside.

To prepare the spicy pepper jelly: Add peppers to a large saucepot. Add vinegars and Old Bay and steep on low heat for 15 minutes. Add sugar, stirring until dissolved. Blend mixture in a blender or using an immersion blender until smooth. Allow to cool slightly and add gelatin and pepper flakes. Chill in the refrigerator until ready to serve.

To prepare the pork chops: Heat a grill to medium. Add pork chops and sear, flipping once, about 4 minutes. Move chops to the cold part of the grill and continue to cook, flipping once, about 6 minutes, or until internal temperature reaches 125°F for medium-rare. Set pork chops aside to rest for 10 minutes.

To serve: Serve pork chops with about 3 ounces each of the bourbon sauce, 2 ounces carrot purée and 1 tablespoon spicy pepper jelly. Serve with additional vegetables, such as roasted carrots and/or turnips, if desired.

Rose Mary

932 W Fulton Street
(872) 260-3921
Rosemarychicago.com

Bravo TV's *Top Chef* (Season 15) winner Joe Flamm opened his highly anticipated restaurant, Rose Mary, in the burgeoning Fulton Market district of Chicago's West Loop neighborhood in April 2021. "Rose Mary is the culmination of everything I have done with my career," says Flamm. "But more importantly, it's the culmination of my personal journey thus far. It's a marriage of who I am, what I've learned, and the person I've built a life and a family with." Named for Flamm's grandmothers, Mary and Mary Rose, and the herb rosemary, which grows natively along the Italian and Croatian coastlines—Rose Mary offers a seasonal menu of rustic yet refined dishes that encapsulate what Flamm has coined "Adriatic drinking food." Blending classic and timeless dishes from his Italian heritage with bold and vibrant flavors from Croatia, where his wife, Hillary is from, Flamm uses a charcoal hearth and an abundance of seasonal ingredients for his menu. Much of Flamm's career, however, is rooted in Italian cooking and technique; his family is from Italy, and he has traveled extensively throughout the country while researching dishes for Spiaggia, the iconic, fine-dining Italian institution formerly owned by Chef Tony Mantuano, where Flamm made a name for himself for the five and a half years he served as executive chef. Prior to Spiaggia,

Flamm worked with many other notable Chicago chefs, but it was in his grandma's kitchen where he first learned to make handmade pasta. These ribs are a nod to the kind of laid-back, family-style food he enjoys serving now. Serve the ribs with just about any grilled vegetable side or a hearty salad and crisp bread for a Mediterranean-inspired meal.

PORK PAMPANELLA RIBS
(SERVES 1-2)

1 rack baby back pork ribs

1 tablespoon fennel pollen

2 teaspoons paprika

2 teaspoon salt

1 teaspoon mustard powder

1 teaspoon dried oregano

2 tablespoons olive oil

2 teaspoons sugar

2 ounces honey

1 tablespoon Calabrian chiles, diced

Preheat a smoker or grill to 300°F.

Pat pork dry with paper towels. In a small bowl, mix together the fennel, paprika, salt, mustard, oregano and sugar. Rub ribs with the spice mixture.

Smoke or grill ribs until tender for 1½ hours. Remove and drizzle olive oil over the ribs.

Wrap in foil and smoke or grill until tender, about another 1½ hour.

Add honey and Calabrian chiles to a small saucepan and bring to a boil over medium heat. Remove from heat and let steep for 5 minutes.

Drizzle the honey mixture over the ribs and serve immediately, slicing in half for 2 servings.

THE GAGE, ACANTO, BEACON TAVERN

24 S Michigan Avenue
(312) 372-4243
Thegagechicago.com

18 S Michigan Avenue
(312) 578-0763
Acantochicago.com

405 N Wabash Avenue
(312) 955-4226

Chef Chris Gawronski, who now helms the kitchen at The Gage, Acanto and Beacon Tavern, joined Gage Hospitality Group in March 2011 as chef de cuisine for the former Henri (now Acanto). Growing up in Michigan, he learned the ins and outs of the kitchen from an early age. His father, a Master Chef, owned Italian restaurants where pasta was made from scratch, including his favorite, rotelle, or as Gawronski called it as a child "wagon wheels and red sauce." Gawronski began his culinary career in Columbus, Ohio, before moving to Los Angeles, where he held positions at several acclaimed and Michelin star-awarded restaurants. These eggs—a favorite among many at The Gage—can be baked in the oven, if one does not own a fryer (or does not wish to hassle with deep fat frying), but they will not be quite as golden brown or crispy. In the restaurant, Gawronski uses hard-cooked eggs because they are more user-friendly and better suited to higher volumes, but at home he prefers to use a soft- or medium-cooked egg. The recipe calls for 10 eggs because soft- and medium-cooked eggs do have a tendency to rip open while being peeled, so there might be some lost. For a hard-cooked egg, increase the simmer time to 10 minutes, for a soft cooked egg (my favorite) decrease the cook time to 6.5 minutes and be gentle while peeling.

SCOTCH EGGS WITH SALAD AND MUSTARD VINAIGRETTE

(SERVES 6)

For the scotch eggs:

10 large eggs, divided

3 quarts water

¼ cup white vinegar

1 pound bulk pork sausage (such as hot or mild Italian-style, or breakfast-style)

1 cup all-purpose flour

½ teaspoon salt

½ teaspoon freshly ground black pepper

⅛ teaspoon cayenne

2 to 4 cups panko breadcrumbs

Canola or other high-heat, neutral oil, for frying

Whole grain mustard, for garnish (optional)

For the salad with mustard vinaigrette:

¼ cup vinegar (red wine, apple cider, champagne, sherry, etc.)

1 tablespoon Dijon mustard

1 tablespoon pure maple syrup or honey

1 teaspoon dried thyme or 2 teaspoons chopped fresh thyme leaves

Salt, to taste

Freshly ground black pepper, to taste

¾ cup extra-virgin olive oil

To prepare the scotch eggs: In a medium saucepan, bring water and vinegar to a simmer. Gently drop the eggs into the simmering water and cook for 6½ minutes for soft-boiled and 8 minutes for

medium. Remove the cooked eggs using a slotted spoon and drain on a paper towel-lined plate. Let cool for 5 to 10 minutes. When cool enough to handle, gently peel off the shell. Transfer the peeled eggs to the refrigerator to cool completely.

Meanwhile, divide the sausage into 6 balls, about 2½ inches each. In the palm of your hand, flatten each of the sausage balls into a 5-inch disk. Wrap one of the disks completely around one of the eggs, doing your best to seal and smooth the edges. None of the egg white should be showing through the sausage. Repeat with rest of sausage and eggs. Place the eggs on a plate and freeze for 20 to 30 minutes. The sausage needs to be fairly firm before breading.

Mix together the flour, salt, black pepper and cayenne in a shallow bowl. In another shallow bowl, beat the remaining 4 eggs. Place the panko in another shallow bowl. To bread the sausage-wrapped eggs, dip the eggs, one at a time, in the flour mixture, then in the egg mixture, then in the panko, shaking to remove excess. To avoid getting breading-coated fingers, use one of your hands to handle the dry ingredients and one hand for the wet. Allow the coated eggs to rest for at least 15 minutes before frying, so the breading will have time to adhere.

To fry the eggs*, pour oil into a large saucepot to cover at least 4 inches of the sides of the pot, with about 4 to 6 inches of clearance above the oil to prevent the hot oil from boiling over. Heat oil to 350°F.

One by one, lower the eggs into the oil and fry them until the breadcrumb layer is golden brown, about 3 to 5 minutes. Transfer the eggs to a paper towel-lined tray using a slotted spoon. Place the eggs in a 350°F oven for 5 to 10 minutes to ensure the sausage has cooked and the egg has heated through. The internal temperature of the egg should read 140°F to 145°F.

Transfer eggs to an ice bath to cool.

To prepare the salad: Add the vinegar, mustard, maple syrup, thyme, salt and pepper to the bottom of a large mixing or salad bowl. Whisk to combine. While whisking, add the oil until creamy. Add the greens and gently toss to coat.

To serve: Divide salad among 6 plates. Slice eggs in half or in quarters and serve atop the salads. Serve with extra whole-grain mustard on the side, if desired.

*If you do not have access to a fryer, these eggs can be baked in the oven, but note they will not be as browned or crispy. Place the breaded eggs on a baking tray and bake for 20 to 30 minutes at 375°F. Turn the eggs every 10 minutes to ensure even cooking.

POULTRY

Serious, old-school restaurant critics and food connoisseurs would say never order chicken breast at a restaurant, on account of the dreaded dryness. Nowadays, with better access to smaller-production, sustainable, family farms and the top chefs here to cook it, no chicken part need go uneaten. Today, as fried chicken and other comfort staples have made a comeback, chefs are keeping it classy and adding their own creative spins. From the many fried chicken renditions—from nachos to mac n' cheese at Honey Butter Fried Chicken and the wood-roasted local chicken used in Chef Rick Bayless' fame tacos—chicken in all its various forms has become a mainstay on menus around town.

Frontera Grill/Topolobampo/Xoco

445 North Clark Street, River North
(312) 661-1434
Fronterakitchens.com

If Diana Kennedy is the abuela or grandmother of authentic Mexican cuisine in the United States, Rick Bayless is the abuelo of fine-dining Mexican. Now a household name, revered both domestically and abroad, Bayless first learned and loved authentic Mexican cuisine studying Latin American culture at the University of Oklahoma, and later while working on a doctorate in anthropological linguistics at the University of Michigan.

But it wasn't until he traveled to and lived in Mexico with his wife, business partner, and "rock" Deann that he truly understood and became passionate about its people and cuisine. During a recent trip to central Mexico, his zeal could be witnessed firsthand when Bayless lit up like a kid in a candy store at the small town's open-air market, enthusiastically explaining different ingredients and thinking up ways to use them for a cooking demonstration later that afternoon. Even in this rural Mexico town, many fans ran up to greet him.

Bayless grew up working in his parents' barbecue restaurant in Oklahoma City. So it wasn't a surprise that he turned to a life of cooking and restaurant ownership. But before that, he'd become an author, developing the masterpiece that is *Authentic Mexican: Regional Cooking from the Heart of Mexico* with Deann. Mexican cooking sealed the deal. Bayless ultimately moved to Chicago, where he opened Frontera Grill in 1987 and, two years later, the more fine-dining-focused Topolobampo next door, becoming one of the most celebrated chefs in the nation.

At a time when fine dining in Chicago was predominantly French, Bayless asked, why not Mexican—the same techniques were used in regional Mexican cooking, elevated by precision, creativity, and artfulness in plating and presentation. It was and still is a team effort in the kitchens at Topolobampo and Frontera Grill, which for eleven years included right-hand man and chef de cuisine Brian Enyart, who recently stepped down. Everything is talked about, ideas shared, tested, tweaked, and tested some more before ever hitting the menu, especially at fine-dining Topolobampo. Nothing is hurried, nothing is just OK or passable. At the same time, all the food is approachable and accessible to everyone. These are the first restaurants of their kind, not just for Chicago but for the country. It's no wonder lines form outside the restaurants well before the doors open and prime-time reservations can take months to get.

But Bayless isn't just a chef; he's an educator at heart. While researching his book, he hosted a television series on regional Mexican cooking. Now he continues his television work, producing and hosting the PBS series *Mexico: One Plate at a Time,* often cooking, traveling, and teaching alongside daughter Lanie, with whom he's also coauthored a book. Outside of that, Bayless continues to host demonstrations, lectures, and other events geared to teaching the everyday American consumer about Mexican culture and cuisine. There was once a time when average home cooks couldn't buy a jalapeño in Chicago, and even if they could, they wouldn't know what to do with it. Now that seems impossible to imagine, and it's fair to say that Bayless had something to do with it.

One of the endeavors Bayless says he's most proud of is his establishment of the Frontera Farmer Foundation, a charitable organization dedicated to supporting Chicago-area family farms. Bayless has been a longtime supporter of "the little guy" when it comes to ingredient sourcing and supplying, and this extends back to the late eighties and early nineties. "I was fortunate to have someone like Rick be so encouraging and supportive," says Tracey Vowell of Three Sisters Garden in Kankakee, Illinois, who managed both restaurant kitchens for six years and slowly made the transition to farming. "I had to make sure I had a stable income throughout the change, and Rick was interested in keeping me around and using products from the farm. Rick was very kind the way he let me sort of wander off—it was a good relationship."

Bayless is a grower too, planting his own herbs, vegetables, and fruits in his home's expansive garden for his personal use as well as for the restaurant. Then there are the charitable activities, the endless cookbooks, and the line of jarred salsas, seasonings, and more under the Frontera Foods label, a business venture Deann Bayless started and continues to run. It's a restaurant enterprise that shows no signs of slowing down anytime soon.

That includes Bayless's latest concept, XOCO, a street-food-focused carryout and casual dine-in eatery next to Topolobampo that was an instant success when it opened in 2009 with a menu heavy on breakfast and lunch tortas and soups, all made with locally sourced foods, of course. On top of that, Bayless still found time to participate in Bravo TV's *Top Chef Masters* show and win. The Top Chef Master title really does say it all.

CARNITAS DE PATO (CHUNKS OF DUCK MEAT) WITH CRUNCHY TOMATILLO-AVOCADO SALSA

(MAKES 3 GENEROUS CUPS OF CARNITAS AND 2½ CUPS OF SALSA)

For the duck carnitas:

6 large duck legs (about 2½–3 pounds total)

4 teaspoons salt

2 teaspoons dried oregano, preferably Mexican

2 tablespoons freshly squeezed lime juice

6 cups fresh lard

8 garlic cloves, peeled and halved

For the tomatillo-avocado salsa:

4 medium tomatillos, husks removed, rinsed

½ cup loosely packed, coarsely chopped cilantro

2 small serrano chiles, stemmed and roughly chopped

¼ cup water

1 ripe avocado, peeled and pitted

1 small white onion, cut into ¼-inch dice

¾ teaspoon salt, or to taste

For serving:

Fresh tortillas*

To prepare the duck: Marinate the duck. Lay the legs in a 13 x 9-inch nonaluminum baking dish. Season on both sides with the salt, oregano, and lime juice. Cover and refrigerate for at least an hour, up to overnight.

Preheat the oven to 300°F. In a large (4-quart) saucepan, melt the lard. Remove the duck from the baking dish and pat dry with paper towels. Rinse and dry the baking dish. Replace the legs in the dish and cover with melted lard, submerging completely. Scatter the garlic cloves over the duck, nestling them into the lard. Slide into the oven (on a rimmed baking sheet to avoid spills), and bake for about 2 hours, or until duck is very tender. Cool to lukewarm.

To prepare the salsa: Roughly chop 2 of the tomatillos and scoop them into a food processor with the cilantro and chiles. Pour in ¼ cup water and process to a slushy, coarse puree. Roughly chop half the avocado, add it to the processor, and pulse until it is incorporated into the salsa. Scrape into a serving dish. Rinse diced onion in cold water, drain, and add to the salsa. Finely chop the remaining tomatillos and add to salsa. Finally, chop the remaining avocado into ¼-inch pieces and stir them into the salsa, along with the salt.

Once duck is cool enough, remove from the lard. Pull off the skin and set aside. Pull off the meat in large pieces, discarding the bones. In a very large (12-inch) skillet, heat 2 tablespoons of the lard over medium-high heat. When lard is hot but not smoking, add the duck skin and cook, turning frequently, until very crisp, about 5 minutes. Remove and drain on paper towels. Next, add the meat and cook, turning regularly, until browned and crisping in spots, about 7 or 8 minutes. Drain on paper towels. Scoop onto a serving platter, coarsely crumbling the duck skin over the top. Serve with the tomatillo-avocado salsa and warm tortillas.

*While homemade tortillas are ideal, to quickly warm store-bought tortillas without drying them out, Bayless recommends wrapping a small stack in a damp towel or damp paper towel and microwaving for 30 seconds on full power. Transfer tortillas to a tortilla warmer. These warmers can be made out of ceramic, stone, plastic, or hand-woven straw and/or cloth, some versions of which are also microwave friendly.

Le Colonial

937 North Rush Street, Gold Coast
(312) 255-0088
Lecolonialchicago.com

This French-Vietnamese institution in Chicago's Gold Coast neighborhood is a celebrity-sighting jackpot. Countless stars, from actors and musicians to politicians and other movers and shakers, have taken seats here, both inside and out on the charming sidewalk patio during fairer weather months. Le Colonial's winning combination of good food and literally dramatic ambience in a prime location has kept it alive through growing competition, recessions, and other typical restaurant challenges.

Tucked between nightclubs, big scenester restaurants, and trendy boutiques on this busy stretch of Rush Street, Le Colonial sits just south of the Rush and State Street intersection, infamously known as the "Viagra Triangle," which earned its nickname from the many affluent, luxury-car-driving men seeking women in the area.

Le Colonial stands apart from the rest of this street as a quiet, serene oasis, thanks to a bright and breezy dining room with tall green ferns, light ivory walls covered in mirrors, and French doors that open on warm days. When it comes to the menu, many say Le Colonial was the first of its kind in the city, serving a fine-dining version of the Vietnamese classics typically found farther

north in Little Vietnam, elevated by high-quality ingredients and gorgeous, almost sultry plating. The Ca Chien Saigon, crispy seared whole red snapper, and Sup Do Bien, a Vietnamese fish stew in a lemongrass saffron broth, rank as the most popular dishes. Here chef Chan Le offers a recipe for another lemongrass-broth–based dish typically found in Vietnamese cuisine.

GA XAO XA OT (SPICY LEMONGRASS CHICKEN)
(SERVES 3)

10 ounces sliced chicken breast

2 tablespoons cornstarch

¼ cup canola oil, divided

2 portobello caps, cleaned

3 tablespoons fish sauce

4½ teaspoons oyster sauce

2 tablespoons sugar

1 stalk lemongrass, bottom only, sliced*

2 cloves garlic, chopped

¾ teaspoon red chile pepper flakes

6 Asian basil leaves, stacked, rolled into a cigar shape, and thinly sliced

Preheat the oven to 350°F.

Combine the chicken, cornstarch, and 2 tablespoons of the oil in a resealable plastic bag or bowl to marinate. Refrigerate.

Brush portobello caps lightly with 1 tablespoon oil and roast in the oven for 15 minutes. When cool enough to handle, slice caps into 1½-inch pieces and set aside.

Next, prepare the sauce. Combine the fish and oyster sauces and sugar in a small bowl; set aside.

Heat 1 tablespoon oil in a wok or deep sauté pan over medium-high heat. When oil begins to shimmer, add the chicken and cook, tossing frequently, until browned and almost cooked through, about 4–5 minutes. Add the lemongrass, garlic, and red pepper flakes and cook until fragrant, tossing frequently, about 1 minute. Add the portobello caps and the sauce. Continue to cook, tossing frequently until liquid has reduced slightly, about another 1–2 minutes. Garnish with basil and serve.

*To prepare the lemongrass, first cut off the top two-thirds, the green part, leaving about a 4-inch white-only stalk. Next, make a thin slit down the stalk and peel away the tough outer layers. Slice the remaining stalk into ¼-inch pieces.

SUMMER HOUSE

1954 N Halsted Street
(773) 634-4100
Summerhouserestaurants.com

Amid the breezy, Orange County vibes of Summer House Santa Monica, Executive Chef Ben Goodnick helms the kitchen, drawing inspiration from California-coastal cuisine. As a divisional chef with Lettuce Entertain You Enterprises, Goodnick also oversees Stella Barra, a pizza concept, with locations next to Summer House in Chicago as well as in Bethesda, Maryland, and Santa Monica and Hollywood, California. A Southern Illinois native, Goodnick began his culinary career at 18, when he moved to Chicago and began working his way up the ranks of many of the city's most renowned restaurants. While attending classes at the former Cooking and Hospitality Institute of Chicago (CHIC), he earned street cred by manning the garde manger station at the now-closed, suburban nouveau French institution Carlos'. Shortly thereafter, Goodnick began his lengthy tenure with LEYE, first working as tournant at acclaimed Chef Gabino Sotelino's outpost Ambria before being promoted to sous chef at Ambria's little sister, Mon Ami Gabi. It was here that he worked closely with Chef/Partner Susan Weaver whom he credits with helping him become the collaborative chef he is today. After a brief stint on the East Coast in the mid-2000s, he returned to Chicago to take over as head chef back at Mon Ami. In 2012, he opened the first

Beatrix location in River North Chicago, working closely with a small LEYE team. He took the helm at Summer House a year later. Here is his recipe for an easy, no-fail roast chicken that goes well with just about any vegetable or side of choice.

SANTA MONICA'S WHOLE ROASTED CHICKEN
(SERVES 3-4)

1 whole chicken (about 4 pounds)

3 tablespoons butter, softened

1 teaspoon finely chopped fresh thyme leaves (plus more for garnish) or ½ teaspoon dried thyme

1 teaspoon brown sugar

2 large yellow onions, peeled, quartered

½ teaspoon salt, or to taste

¼ teaspoon freshly ground black pepper, or to taste

Preheat the oven to 425°F.

In a small bowl, mix together the butter, thyme, brown sugar, salt and pepper.

Place the onions in a 9 x 13-inch baking dish. Place the chicken, breast side up, in the center over the onions.

Using your fingers, gently separate the skin from the breast. Rub half of the butter mixture between the skin and breast. Carefully push some of the butter between the skin and meat of the legs. Dot the rest of the butter over the onions. Sprinkle the chicken and onions with extra salt and pepper, if desired.

Roast the chicken for 50 to 60 minutes, or until a meat thermometer inserted into the thickest part of the thigh registers 165°F.

Let the chicken rest for 10 minutes before carving and serving. Serve on a platter with the onions and extra fresh thyme leaves, if using.

HBFC

3361 N Elston Avenue
(773) 478-4000
Honeybutter.com

Chefs Joshua Kulp and Christine Cikowski opened Honey Butter Fried Chicken in 2013 after many years of success with Sunday Night Dinner Club, their "underground" dinner party hosted out of Cikowski's apartment, and after drawing hungry Green City Market shoppers to their regular Saturday stand where they served up their famous Midwest burgers using all ingredients from local farmers, meat producers and cheesemongers. For their first restaurant, they zeroed in on one of their most popular dinner club dishes— fried chicken slathered with honey butter (on the chicken, not on the cornbread side). In the first week (and continuing for months on end), when Honey Butter Fried Chicken opened, lines wrapped around the block. While running the successful restaurant, the duo didn't close their underground dinner party completely; it continues upstairs as a catering and special events operation with a rotating menu. In addition to serving highly addictive food, Kulp and Cikowski have served as a beacon for those seeking work and as a model operation for other chefs and restaurateurs in the city thanks to bottom-up (not top-down, brigade culture) policy that pays employees competitive wages, plus ben-

efits, which they developed after an intensive training seminar held at Zingerman's in Ann Arbor, Michigan, by the progressive and positive-culture-driven business owner Ari Weinzweig. Here is the recipe for their much-coveted fried chicken in the form of a zippy mac n' cheese. If you're at the restaurant, pick up a bag of Honey Butter Fried Chicken Flour Mix and use that in place of the seasoned flour mix below.

BUFFALO MAC N' CHEESE WITH CHICKEN CRUNCHIES

(SERVES 4)

For the brine and chicken:

⅓ cup coarse kosher salt

¼ cup granulated sugar

⅛ teaspoon red chile pepper flakes

2 quarts water

Peel of one lemon

Peel of one orange

2 boneless skinless chicken thighs

2 boneless, skin-on split breasts, cut in half crosswise

2 drumsticks

For the seasoned flour and dredge:

1¾ cups unbleached, all-purpose flour

¼ cup rice flour

1½ teaspoons coarse kosher salt, plus more for garnishing the chicken

1½ teaspoons freshly ground black pepper

1½ teaspoons garlic powder

1 teaspoon onion powder

¼ teaspoon baking powder

⅛ teaspoon cayenne pepper

⅛ teaspoon smoked paprika, plus more for garnishing the chicken

1 quart buttermilk

Canola, rice bran or peanut oil, for frying

To prepare the brine: Combine the salt, sugar, red chile flakes, water, lemon and orange peel in a large pot and heat over medium heat, stirring until sugar and salt dissolve. Cool the brine completely.

To prepare the chicken: Place the chicken pieces in brine and refrigerate for 8 to 12 hours. Remove chicken from the brine and pat dry with paper towels.

To prepare batter for the chicken: Place the flour, rice flour, salt, pepper, garlic powder, onion powder, baking powder, cayenne and smoked paprika in a wide container and stir to combine. Pour the

buttermilk into a second container. Batter each piece of chicken one at a time. Submerge the chicken first in buttermilk. Lift the chicken out of the buttermilk, and let drip slightly, and place into chicken dredge flour container and coat the chicken again. Be careful to ensure that the chicken is evenly and fully coated, but do not let the coating become too thick. Place the battered chicken onto a plate and proceed with battering the remaining chicken.

To fry the chicken: Pour enough oil in a wide, deep skillet or Dutch oven to reach 4 inches along the sides. Heat oil over medium heat to 340°F. Working in 2 batches, place the chicken gently into the hot oil. Carefully adjust the heat to keep the oil at a constant 315 to 320°F. Fry the chicken until each piece reads at least 165°F at its thickest point. When the chicken is cooked, remove carefully from the oil and place on a wire rack over a cookie sheet or on paper towels.

When cooled, dust the top side of the just fried chicken with a sprinkle of salt and a sprinkle of smoked paprika. Let rest for one minute, flip the chicken and dust the other side with salt and smoked paprika. Serve with Honey Buffalo Pimento Mac N' Cheese.*

---

*HONEY BUFFALO PIMENTO MAC N' CHEESE

For the mac n' cheese:

8 ounces sharp cheddar cheese spread

3 tablespoons buttermilk

⅓ cup pimento or roasted red peppers, pureed and strained

Kosher salt and freshly ground black pepper

2 or 3 fresh scallions green parts, thinly sliced, for garnish

For the honey buffalo sauce:

1 cup hot sauce (such as Crystal brand)

1 tablespoon cornstarch

1 tablespoon water

¼ cup honey

¼ cup unsalted butter, diced

Kosher salt and freshly ground black pepper

To prepare the Honey Buffalo Sauce: Bring the hot sauce to a boil. In a bowl, whisk the water and cornstarch together, and add to hot sauce. Bring the mixture back up to a boil and continue to whisk until thickened. Turn off the heat and whisk in the honey. Slowly whisk the butter into the hot sauce, a couple pieces at a time. Season with salt and pepper to taste. Set aside.

To prepare the Mac n' Cheese: Warm the cheese and buttermilk in a small saucepot over medium heat just until cheese melts into the buttermilk.

Whisk cheese sauce and pimento puree and mix occasionally until the ingredients are well incorporated. Season with salt and pepper to taste.

To serve: Divide the mac n' cheese between 4 wide bowls or on plates. Chop the fried chicken into 1- inch pieces and arrange over the top of the mac and cheese. Spoon honey buffalo sauce over both. Garnish with scallions.

superkhana international

3059 W Diversey Avenue
(773) 661-9028
Superkhanachicago.com

Chefs Yoshi Yamada and Zeeshan Shah drew an immediate following for this dish at their first restaurant venture, Superkhana International, which celebrates a mashup of Indian, Italian and other cuisines. The duo draws from Yamada's Japanese and Italian heritage and Shah's paternal Indian heritage (with the backing of longtime Lula Café chef/owner and award-winning Jason Hammel) at Superkhana, where they have looked to "create a fun, energetic and welcoming place where we can cook what we always wanted to cook," says Yamada. "We love Indian food and wanted to present it with a breadth of flavors and styles of cuisine." The results are magnificent!

BUTTER CHICKEN NAAN CALZONE
(SERVES 8)

For the butter chicken:

3 tablespoons Desi or plain whole-milk yogurt

2½ tablespoons butter chicken spice blend (or a blend of ½ tablespoon haidi, 1 tablespoon daniya and 1 tablespoon jeera)

1 tablespoon grapeseed or neutral oil

1 teaspoon freshly squeezed lemon juice

1 pound boneless, skinless chicken thighs

For the butter chicken gravy:

2 tablespoons grapeseed oil

1 cup thinly sliced white onion

3 tablespoons minced ginger

4 tablespoons minced garlic

¼ teaspoon ground clove

½ teaspoon cinnamon

1 teaspoon salt

2 tablespoons tomato paste

1½ teaspoons granulated sugar

1 cup chicken stock

1½ cups undrained canned whole tomatoes

½ cup heavy cream

1 stick (½ cup) butter

¼ teaspoon Methi (Optional)

For the calzone:

2½ pounds fresh prepared pizza dough, at room temperature

3 ounces Amul cheese, shredded (about ¾ cup)

¾ cup shredded mozzarella cheese

All-purpose flour, for dusting

1 large egg, beaten

1½ tablespoons melted ghee or butter

Flaky sea salt, for garnish

To prepare the butter chicken: Stir together the yogurt, spices, oil and lemon juice in a large bowl. Add chicken, turning to coat. Cover and refrigerate for at least 1 hours or up to 3 hours.

Drain chicken from the marinade. Roll up each thigh and place together snuggly to completely fill out a roasting or baking pan.

Cook the chicken uncovered for 45 to 60 minutes until internal temperature reaches higher than normal, about 200°F. This will break down the connective tissue of the thigh without drying out the chicken. Be careful not to burn exposed chicken, turning the chicken if it gets too much color on one side.

To prepare the butter chicken gravy: Heat oil in a medium skillet. Add onions and cook until caramelized, stirring occasionally, about 10 minutes. Add ginger and garlic and cook until fragrant, 1 to 2 minutes. Add clove and cinnamon and cook until flavors have melded, adding a small amount

of water to keep spices from burning, if necessary, about 2 to 3 minutes. Add tomato paste, sugar, salt, stock and tomatoes. Cook until reduced by about ¼ or ⅓ and thickened, stirring regularly. Remove from heat and add cream, butter and Methi, stirring until melted.

Transfer mixture to a blender or, using a handheld immersion blender, blend until smooth. Transfer to the refrigerator to cool (can be made up to 3 hours ahead or refrigerated up to 3 days ahead).

Once the chicken is cooked and cool enough to touch, pick apart the chicken thighs with your hands into chunks, discarding any cartilage or connective tissue. Set aside.

To prepare the calzones: Cut the pizza dough into 8 (5-ounce) pieces and shape each into a ball. Loosely cover dough with plastic wrap and let stand at room temperature for about 30 minutes.

Preheat the oven to 500°F.

Place a pizza stone on a rack on the lowest level of the oven. Preheat the stone for 1 hour. Make sure fan is at high heat. While stone is preheating, take the gravy out of the refrigerator to allow it to come to room temperature. Toss Amul and mozzarella cheeses together and set aside.

Working with one dough ball at a time, place the proofed dough on a lightly floured work surface. Roll or stretch each ball into an 8-inch disc. Place about ⅓ cup each of butter chicken gravy and shredded chicken on one half of the disc, away from the edge by the width of a finger. Top with a couple tablespoons of the cheese mixture. Fold the other half over the filling. Seal the edge by pressing down with your finger to close, then "braid" the sealed edge by folding it over on itself around the curved rim. Brush gently with the melted ghee or butter.

Working with 1 or 2 prepared calzones at a time, slide the calzones off the lightly floured peel onto the hot pizza stone and close the oven immediately. Cook for 6 minutes uninterrupted. When the calzone is brown and golden, with little whiteness to the bread, it is ready to be removed. Otherwise, continue to bake, checking at 1-minute increments. Brush the top of the calzone with melted ghee and sprinkle a pinch of finishing salt on top.

DESSERT

A restaurant meal is never complete without a little sweet treat at the end. Chicago's pastry chefs have garnered so much attention over the years that they've made names for themselves in their own right. The best are quickly gobbled up by the big restaurant groups and hotels. Others have partnered with chefs and spouses to create savory-sweet collaborations. Now it's not uncommon to see the pastry chef just as celebrated and revered as the executive chef. If the last bite is just as important as the first at a restaurant because of the lasting impression it leaves, so should it be at home, and especially when entertaining friends and family. Life is too short, as they say: eat cake.

MINDY'S BAKERY

1747 N Damen Avenue
(773) 489-1747
Mindysbakery.com (Temporarily closed)

Famed Pastry Chef and Baker Mindy Segal closed her namesake sit-down restaurant, Mindy's Hot Chocolate, after 15 years in 2020 to make room for a more casual outpost as Mindy's Bakery, offering a wide assortment of baked goods, from bagels to challah, cookies and more. Segal's philosophy as a chef is to source the best possible ingredients, from chocolate to flour, but she remains most committed to supporting local farms. A graduate of Kendall College in Chicago, Segal trained in the legendary kitchens of Charlie Trotter's and the former Spago and Gordon before teaming up with Michael Kornick to helm the sweet side of his iconic restaurant MK. In recent years, Segal has also branched into the cannabis sector, developing her popular and artisanal, cannabis-infused gummies, which are available at local dispensaries. This recipe, which relies on seasonal, local ingredients, is a throwback to her finer-dining days of yore and offers a healthier "doughnut" in the form of a carved-out peach. If you happen to have a crème brulee handheld blowtorch, caramelize the sabayon (custard) for a few seconds. You may also substitute the verjuice for a good-quality, white wine vinegar spiked with a drop or two of freshly squeezed lemon juice.

GRILLED MARINATED DOUGHNUT PEACHES WITH LEMON SABAYON AND POACHED MICHIGAN BLUEBERRIES

(SERVES 6)

For the peaches and blueberries:

6 doughnut peaches, pitted

½ cup peach liqueur or sweet dessert wine

1 tablespoon sugar

1 vanilla bean, split lengthwise

1 tablespoon verjuice

1 pinch cracked black pepper

For the lemon sabayon:

2 eggs

2 egg yolks

¼ cup granulated sugar

1 tablespoon water

⅓ cup freshly squeezed lemon juice

1 pint fresh blueberries

To prepare the peaches: In a large bowl, combine liqueur, sugar, vanilla bean, verjuice, and pepper. Add peaches, tossing to coat. Let stand at room temperature, 1 hour. Before serving, prepare a grill at medium heat. Drain peaches, reserving liquid. Grill peaches, flipping occasionally until tender and slightly caramelized on both sides.

To prepare the sabayon: Whisk together the eggs, yolks, sugar, water, and lemon juice in a large stainless-steel bowl or in the upper pot of a double boiler. Over simmering water, whisk custard until thick and tripled in volume. When custard is thickened, set bowl or pot over a bowl of ice and stir occasionally until cool. Set aside.

To poach the blueberries: Pour reserved peach liquid into a shallow saucepan and bring to a boil. Turn heat down to a simmer, add blueberries, and continue to simmer very gently until tender, about 5–7 minutes.

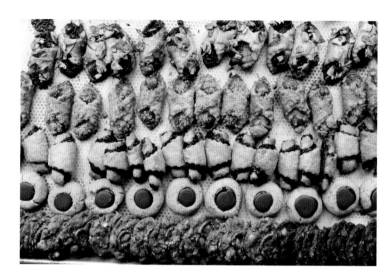

To serve: Divide warm, grilled peaches among shallow bowls or ramekins. In the center of each peach, place a tablespoon of blueberries with liquid. Top with sabayon. If available, use a blowtorch to caramelize the custard brûlée-style. Serve immediately.

ROBERT ET FILS

4229 N Lincoln Avenue
(773) 687-9179
Robertetfilsrestaurant.com

Robert Et Fils, pronounced "Robair Ay Feese," translates to "Robert and son" and is named for Owner and Executive Chef Rob Shaner's late father, whose job took the family from the Midwest to France. Joining him are Pastry Chef Cati Molnar and General Manager Rami Ezza, who grew up in Paris and coincidentally attended the same high school as Shaner in Paris (they discovered this while working in restaurants together throughout Chicago). Shaner dreamed for years about opening a restaurant that captures the unique experience of a bygone era of dining in France. Molnar carries on that tradition at Shaner's North Center neighborhood restaurant, with her freshly baked, naturally-leavened breads using locally-milled flour as well as pastries and classic French desserts. The Ohio native was a school psychologist in Cincinnati when she met Chef Steven Geddes of the farm-to-table restaurant Local 127. Coming from a food-loving family of farmers and Italian and Hungarian immigrants, Molnar felt at home in the restaurant's kitchen, continuing to build her pastry arts skills at sister restaurants Boca and Sotto and Horseshoe Casino Cincinnati before moving to Chicago in 2017 for a job at The Kennison, where she met Shaner and the rest is history.

FRENCH APPLE CAKE
(MAKES 8-12 SLICES OR 16 SQUARE PIECES)

1 cup (120 grams) all-purpose flour

1 teaspoon (4 grams) baking powder

2 large eggs (100 grams)

¾ cup plus 2 tablespoons (150 grams plus 25 grams) sugar

1½ teaspoons (6 grams) salt plus a pinch

3 tablespoons (42 grams) dark rum*

Scant ½ cup (99 g) crème fraîche

4 tablespoons (56 grams) butter, melted

4 large apples (550-600 grams), thinly sliced

Preheat the oven to 375°F. Butter an 8-inch round or square cake pan and line it with parchment paper. Make sure the parchment sits higher than the edges of the pan to make the cake easier to remove when baked and cooled.

Whisk together the flour and baking powder in a medium bowl and set it aside.

In a large bowl, whisk the eggs with ¾ cup of the sugar and the salt until light and foamy, about 2 minutes by hand.

Add the rum and crème fraîche and whisk until evenly combined.

Add the flour and then the melted butter, whisking until just combined into a smooth, even batter.

Gently fold in the apple slices until they are coated in the batter.

Pour the mixture into the prepared pan and smooth the top with a rubber spatula. Sprinkle remaining sugar and a pinch of salt evenly over the pan.

Bake until set and lightly browned, about 45 to 60 minutes. The cake may sink slightly in the center as it cools.

Cool completely. Lift cake out of the pan and cut into 8 or 12 triangle or 16 (2-inch) squares to serve.

*Brandy, whiskey, or bourbon can be substituted for the rum. For an alcohol-free option, use 4 teaspoons (19 g) vanilla extract and increase crème fraîche to a full ½ cup (113 g).

Dear Margaret

2965 N Lincoln Avenue
(773) 360-8213
Dearmargaretchi.com

Chef Ryan Brosseau worked in the kitchens at some of Chicago's best restaurants before opening his own outpost, Dear Margaret, with business partner Lacey Irby, in the midst of the 2020 coronavirus pandemic—no small feat when they had to start with takeout only. Now, with only 14 seats total, Brosseau and his team are able to greet guests in the dining room for a dinner party feel. Immediately upon opening, the restaurant, tucked in an intimate storefront in the residential West Lakeview neighborhood, quickly earned accolades, most notably for its both inventive and traditional dishes inspired by Brosseau's Canadian roots. This recipe fits that mold as a quintessential

Canadian dessert. "Butter tarts are essentially a sugar custard in the same style as a pecan pie or chess pie," Brosseau says. "I used to eat them as a kid, and those usually included raisins and sometimes walnuts." The version at Dear Margaret has dried blueberries, which is Brosseau's favorite fruit, and he bakes them in a butter-lard crust using individual tart pans, but you can also bake the tarts using a muffin tin pan, like how his grandmother baked the dessert.

BUTTER TARTS
(MAKES 8 [2½-INCH] TARTS)

For the sweet pastry crusts:

55 grams all-purpose flour

10 grams sugar

Pinch of salt (heaping ⅛ teaspoon)

30 grams cold unsalted butter (European butter preferred, i.e., Plugra)

15 grams cold lard*

14 mL cold water (as needed)

For the custard filling:

3 large eggs

50 grams unsalted butter, softened (preferably European-style butter)

25 grams light brown sugar (or dark for a richer color and molasses flavor)

125 grams granulated sugar

5 grams vanilla paste

100 grams maple syrup

Dried blueberries (or other dried fruit, such as raisins or currants)

Chopped nuts and/or unsweetened shredded coconut flakes (optional, for garnish)

To prepare the crust: Pulse the flour, sugar and salt in food processor. Add butter and lard, pulsing until pea sized. Add enough water until dough just comes together, pulsing on and off.

Transfer dough to a chopping board and lightly shape into a large ball. Wrap dough in plastic and refrigerate for 1 hour.

Preheat the oven to 350°F (325°F for convection).

Roll dough to ⅛-inch thickness. Cut out circles using 3-inch cutter to fit into 8 (2½-inch) aluminum tart shells or cut into 4-inch circles for lining a standard muffin tin.

To prepare the custard: Purée eggs, butter, light brown sugar, granulated sugar, vanilla paste and maple syrup in a blender until smooth. Alternately, use a hand mixer or stick blender.

Add 5 dried blueberries to the bottom of each crust shell. Cover with about 1 ounce of the custard mix.

Transfer muffin pan to the oven, or place aluminum tart shells on a sheet tray filled with about ½ inch of water. Bake until custard is set, 10-12 minutes.

Remove from the oven and cool completely. Top with additional toppings, such as chopped nuts or shredded, unsweetened coconut, if desired, before serving warm. Tarts can also be refrigerated and served chilled.

*In the pastry crust, if omitting lard, use 450 grams total butter.

SMYTH AND THE LOYALIST

177 N Ada Street #101, #001
(773) 913-3773
Smythandtheloyalist.com

Chefs John and Karen (Urie) Shields worked together under the late, legendary Charlie Trotter before venturing out on their own with their first restaurant in the quaint town of Smyth, Virginia. They had a strong run there, showcasing foods from local farms and drawing a regular following, before returning to the Windy City to grow their family. They opened Smyth and The Loyalist in a two-floor, West Loop space, where The Loyalist would feature a pub-style menu in a more casual, tavern-like space on the lower level, while Smyth, named after their former digs, would serve as the upstairs tasting room showcasing their whimsical creations in an intimate and cozy space with views into the kitchen. John Shields continues to helm the savory side, once even drawing a cult following for The Loyalist's burger, while Karen Shields overlooks the sweet, although both say they collaborate on every dish on the menu, often blending savory and sweet flavors

using the best local ingredients and sustainable fish available. Here, Karen Shields offers her choice for a rich and delicious cake that's always a favorite at the restaurants—it's a labor of love but a standout when served for others.

CHOCOLATE BLACKOUT CAKE
(MAKES ONE 2- OR 3-LAYER CAKE)

For the cake:

2 cups plus 2 tablespoons cake flour, sifted

1¾ cup Dutch-style cocoa, sifted

1 teaspoon salt

1 tablespoon baking powder

1 tablespoon baking soda

3 cups granulated sugar

5 large eggs

1½ cups buttermilk

1 tablespoon vanilla extract

1½ cups hot water, tea or coffee

¾ cups butter, melted

For the chocolate buttercream frosting:

5¾ cups sugar divided by 2¾ cups plus 2 tablespoons sugar

¾ cup egg whites (from about 6 whole eggs)

2 cups unsalted butter, cubed, room temperature

½ cup dark chocolate (64%–72%), melted and cooled

Salt, to taste

To prepare the cake: Add the flour, cocoa, salt, baking powder, baking soda and sugar to a large mixing bowl and set aside.

In a separate, medium bowl, whisk together the eggs, buttermilk and vanilla. Pour the wet ingredients into the dry mix. Add hot water in a slow, steady stream while whisking. Add butter, whisking just to combine.

Preheat the oven to 350°F.

Pour 2 cups of the batter into a 2-inch deep, 9-inch round cake pan for a three-layer cake (or 4 cups for a 4-inch deep, 9-inch round cake pan if making a two-layer cake).

Bake cakes until set and a toothpick inserted in the center comes out clean, about 50 minutes for the 2-inch-deep pans and 60 minutes for the 4-inch pans.

Transfer cake pans to a wire rack and cool completely.

To prepare the buttercream frosting: Whisk egg whites and sugar over a double boiler until sugar is dissolved and mixture is warmed to 140°F. Whip in standing mixer at full speed. Add butter, using paddle to bring together. Fold in melted chocolate.

To frost the cake: Position one of the cakes on a cake stand or plate. Frost the top of the cake, turning to coat with a spatula. Carefully position the second layer over the first and spread more frosting on the top. Add the third layer (if using). Frost the outside of the cake all around, turning to coat evenly. Refrigerate until set, at least 1 hour.

To serve: Slice cake into desired size pieces. Serve with a half scoop of vanilla ice cream, if desired.

Beatrix

519 N Clark Street
(312) 284-1377
Beatrixrestaurants.com

When Lettuce Entertain You Enterprises opened the Beatrix restaurant-meets takeout-meets coffee shop and market concept in 2013, that was a time when gluten-free was beginning to take off in restaurants, with more options for those sensitive or allergic to gluten as well as other allergies. That's when Pastry Chef Yasmin Gutierrez, a graduate of The French Pastry School, who helped open the concept after overseeing LEYE's pastry programs at the former Mity Nice Bar & Grill and Foodlife, came up with this recipe. The Tall, Dark and Handsome is essentially a flourless chocolate cake with a little height and a molten chocolate center, almost like a souffle. Since then, Gutierrez's list of cult favorite desserts has grown to include, most recently, a caramel pie, but she still gets requests for her all-crowd-pleasing dessert. Gutierrez now oversees the pastry program at all four Beatrix locations as well as Beatrix Market and is instrumental with the dessert program at LEYE's Mediterranean restaurants, Aba and Ēma (p. 16).

GLUTEN FREE TALL, DARK AND HANDSOME CHOCOLATE CAKE
(MAKES 1 8-INCH CAKE)

For the cake:

12 ounces dark chocolate pieces or chunks

1 stick (4 ounces) unsalted butter

1 teaspoon vanilla extract

½ teaspoons salt

6 large eggs, separated

5½ ounces granulated sugar, divided

Whipped cream or ice cream, for garnish (optional)

For the filling:

2 cups heavy cream

6.5 ounces dark chocolate pieces or chunks

¾ teaspoon vanilla extract

2.25 ounces granulated sugar

0.5 gram kappa-carrageenan

Preheat the oven to 300°F.

To prepare the cake: Melt the chocolate, butter, vanilla, and salt over a double boiler. Remove from heat and allow to cool slightly.

Separate the egg yolks in a medium mixing bowl and the whites into the bowl of a stand mixer or large mixing bowl.

Whisk the eggs yolk and half of the sugar until pale yellow and thick. Set aside.

Whip the egg whites on low speed (or use a hand-mixer to whisk), until soft peaks form. Slowly add the remaining sugar until medium peaks have formed.

When the chocolate/butter mix has slightly cooled, add 2 tablespoons of the egg yolk mixture to the chocolate mixture, whisking to combine. Add the mixture back to the remaining yolks, whisking until smooth.

Give the mixture several folds with a rubber spatula, then add the egg whites and continue to fold until incorporated.

Immediately pour into a lightly greased, 8-inch cheesecake pan. Bake for 45 minutes. Rotate pan and bake for another 15 minutes. Cake will rise in height and then collapse slightly.

Allow cake to cool until at room temperature. The cake will collapse in the center at this point, creating a hole.

To prepare the filling: In a small bowl, mix together the sugar and kappa-carrageenan and set aside.

Bring the cream, chocolate, and vanilla to a simmer, stirring the entire time, so as not to burn the chocolate.

Whisk in the sugar/carrageenan mixture and continue to whisk for one minute as the cream simmers.

Immediately strain into a container with a spout and pour through the crack in the cakes until ½ inch from the top. Let come to room temperature. Slice cake into 8 pieces and serve with whipped cream or vanilla ice cream, if desired.

PHOTO CREDITS

p. iii, courtesy of Table at Crate; p. v, Vito Palmisano via Getty Images; p. vi, courtesy of Bonhomme Group; pp. xii–xiii, frankcreporter via Getty Images; pp. xiv–1, alvarez via Getty Images; p. 2, 4, courtesy of Regan Baroni; p. 5, courtesy of Sandy Noto; p. 7, courtesy of North Pond; p. 9, bhofack2 via Getty Images; p. 16, 17, courtesy of Jeff Marini; p. 18, courtesy of mfk.; pp. 21, 22, courtesy of Le Sud; p. 24, fcafotodigital via Getty Images; p. 26, courtesy of Light Leak Pictures; p. 28, courtesy of Formento's; p. 30, courtesy of Fisk & Co.; pp. 32, 34, courtesy of Neil Burger; pp. 35, 36, 39, courtesy of Lettuce Entertain You Enterprises (LEYE); p. 40, courtesy of Tree House; p. 42, GMVozd via Getty Images; p. 46, courtesy of Beth Rooney; p. 48, courtesy of Boka Restaurant Group; p. 51, courtesy of Anthony Tahlier; p. 54, courtesy of The Dearborn; pp. 56, 57, 59, courtesy of Osteria Langhe; p. 60, courtesy of The Graceful Ordinary; p. 62, courtesy of Amy Morton; p. 64, courtesy of Hahm Visuals; p. 66, courtesy of Marisa Klug-Morataya (headshot), Jude Goergen (restaurant interior); p. 67, courtesy of Jude Goergen; pp. 68, 69, courtesy of Neil Burger; p. 70, Olivia via Getty Images; p. 72, courtesy of Beth Rooney; p. 74, courtesy of Sarah Stegner; pp. 75, 77, courtesy of Brindille; p. 79, courtesy of Hopleaf; p. 80, courtesy of Michael Salisbury; p. 82, courtesy of Bonhomme Group; p. 84, courtesy of Chez Moi; pp. 86, 87, courtesy of El Che Steakhouse; pp. 88–89, Tatiana Volgutova via Getty Images; p. 90, courtesy of Isabelle Langheim; p. 91, courtesy of Derek Richmond; p. 92, courtesy of The Purple Pig; p. 94, courtesy of Edouard Pierre; pp. 98, courtesy of Conor Rudny; p. 100, courtesy of Arun's; p. 102, courtesy of LEYE; pp. 104, 106, 107, Funkenhausen; p. 107, courtesy of Matt Haas; p. 110, courtesy of The Gage; pp. 112–113, EasyBuy4u via Getty Images; p. 115, courtesy of Beth Rooney; p. 117, courtesy of Beth Rooney; p. 119, courtesy of LEYE; pp. 121, 122, courtesy of Rachel Brown Kulp; pp. 124, 125, 127, courtesy of Belen Aquino; p. 128, Johner Images via Getty Images; pp. 130, 131, 132, courtesy of Mindy Segal; p. 133, courtesy of Lena Jackson; pp. 134, 135, courtesy of Neil Burger; pp. 137, 138, courtesy of Huge Galdones; pp. 139, 140, courtesy of Anjali Pinto; p. 146, courtesy of Bauwerks Photography.

index

A

Aba, 16

Acanto, 109

Agnolotti with Roasted Beets and Pickled Dill, 33

Arun's, 100

avec River North, 80

B

Baby Beet and Farro Salad with Avocado, Tarragon, and Goat's Milk Feta, 12

Bacon-Wrapped Pork Loin Tonnato, 96

Bar Takito, 10

Beacon Tavern, The, 109

Beatnik, 82

Beatrix, 139

Beef

   Beef Tenderloin with Chimichurri, 87

   Curried Meatballs with Avocado Hummus, 83

   Grass-Fed Beef Brisket with Pan-Roasted Parsnips, 73

   Montreal-Style Smoked Brisket Sandwich, 79

Beef Tenderloin with Chimichurri, 87

Big Star, 94

Braised Lamb Shank Mediterranean, 85

Brazilian Cheese Bites, 8

Brindille, 75

Bristol, The, 28

Buffalo Mac n' Cheese with Chicken Crunchies, 122

Butter Basted Monkfish with Kohlrabi, Barley and Green Apple, 63

Butter Chicken Naan Calzone, 125

Butter Tarts, 136

C

Cabra Cevicheria, 48

Café Ba-Ba-Reeba!, 102

Carnitas de Pato (Chunks of Duck Meat) with Crunchy Tomatillo-Avocado Salsa, 116

Chez Moi, 84

Chicago Pizza, 9

Chocolate Blackout Cake, 137

Chorizo-Stuffed Bacon-Wrapped Dates, 90

Cipolla Arrosto, 58

Classic Chicago Steakhouses, 72

Cold Storage, 96

Crab and Lobster Spaghetti, 31

Croquettes with Dijonnaise Dipping Sauce, 22

Curried Meatballs with Avocado Hummus, 83

D

Daisies, 32

Dear Margaret, 135

Dearborn, The, 54

Dessert

   Butter Tarts, 136

   Chocolate Blackout Cake, 137

   French Apple Cake, 133

   Gluten Free Tall, Dark and Handsome Chocolate Cake, 139

   Grilled Marinated Doughnut Peaches with Lemon Sabayon and Poached Michigan Blueberries, 131

Di Pescara, 35

Duck Duck Goat, 48

Duck Egg Carbonara, 29

E

El Che Steakhouse & Bar, 86

Ēma, 16

F

Fish

   Butter Basted Monkfish with Kohlrabi, Barley and Green Apple, 63

   Cipolla Arrosto, 58

   Grilled Swordfish Steak with Fava Bean Smash, Grilled Ramp Vinaigrette, Dates, Frisée and Hearts of Palm Salad, 55

   GT's Clam Chowder, 47

Lobster Esquites, 67

Milk-Poached Cod with White Asparagus and Charred Piquillo Peppers, 52

Mussels with Mighty Goat Sausage, Cilantro Butter, and Bagna Cauda Aioli, 49

Risotto Certosino, 57

Salmon Tartare with Doenjang and Yuzu Crème Fraîche, 65

Shrimp Dejonghe, 69

Steamed Mussels with Lobster Butter Sauce, 61

Wild Striped Bass with Sweet Corn Chowder and Littleneck Clams, 44

Wisconsin Trout Soup with Potato-Infused Cream and Bacon, 53

Fisk & Co, 30

Formento's, 28

French Apple Cake, 133

Frontera Grill, 114

Funkenhausen, 104

G

Ga Xao Xa Ot (Spicy Lemongrass Chicken), 118

Gage, 109

Gaijin, 2

Galit, 5

Girl & the Goat, 48

Gluten Free Tall, Dark and Handsome Chocolate Cake, 139

Graceful Ordinary, The, 60

Grass-Fed Beef Brisket with Pan-Roasted Parsnips, 73

Grilled Marinated Doughnut Peaches with Lemon Sabayon and Poached Michigan Blueberries, 131

Grilled Swordfish Steak with Fava Bean Smash, Grilled Ramp Vinaigrette, Dates, Frisée and Hearts of Palm Salad, 55

GT Fish & Oyster, 46

GT's Clam Chowder, 47

H

Harvest Salad with Quick-Pickled Summer Beans, 3

HBFC, 121

Homemade Labneh (and Whey Brine), 6

Honey Buffalo Pimento Mac n' Cheese, 123

Hopleaf, 78

Hung Lay Curry (turmeric-marinated pork curry), 101

J

Jeong, 64

K

Kimchi Stew with Braised Pork Belly, 99

Kostali, 75

L

La Luna Chicago, 40

Lamb
Braised Lamb Shank Mediterranean, 85

Le Colonial, 117

Le Sud, 21

LeTour, 62

Little Goat, 48

Lobster Esquites, 67

Lula Café, 51

M

Marisol, 51

mfk., 18

Mi Tocaya Antojeria, 66

Milk-Braised Pork Shoulder and Creamy Mashed Potatoes, 93

Milk-Poached Cod with White Asparagus and Charred Piquillo Peppers, 52

Mindy's Bakery, 130

Monteverde, 14

Montreal-Style Smoked Brisket Sandwich, 79

Muhammara, 17

Mussels with Mighty Goat Sausage, Cilantro Butter, and Bagna Cauda Aioli, 49

N

Nonna's, 28

North Pond, 7

O

Okonomiyaki (Savory Japanese Pancake), 4

Osteria Langhe, 56

P

Paella Mixta, 102

Pasta and Noodles
    Agnolotti with Roasted Beets and Pickled Dill, 33
    Crab and Lobster Spaghetti, 31
    Duck Egg Carbonara, 29
    Ravioli Quattro Formaggi (Four Cheese Ravioli), 27
    Rigatoni with Crispy Prosciutto and Vodka Sauce, 41
    Spinach and Ricotta Gnocchi, 36
    Tomato and Summer Squash Gratin, 37

Piccolo Sogno, 26

Pork
    Bacon-Wrapped Pork Loin Tonnato, 96
    Chorizo-Stuffed Bacon-Wrapped Dates, 90
    Curried Meatballs with Avocado Hummus, 83
    Hung Lay Curry (turmeric-marinated pork curry), 101
    Kimchi Stew with Braised Pork Belly, 99
    Milk-Braised Pork Shoulder and Creamy Mashed Potatoes, 93
    Paella Mixta, 102
    Pork Chops with Bourbon Sauce, Carrot Puree and Spicy Pepper Jelly, 105
    Pork Pampanella Ribs, 108
    Scotch Eggs with Salad and Mustard Vinaigrette, 110
    Tacos Al Pastor (Spit-Roasted Pork Tacos), 95

Pork Chops with Bourbon Sauce, Carrot Puree and Spicy Pepper Jelly, 105

Pork Pampanella Ribs, 108

Porto, 82

Poultry
    Buffalo Mac n' Cheese with Chicken Crunchies, 122
    Butter Chicken Naan Calzone, 125
    Carnitas de Pato (Chunks of Duck Meat) with Crunchy Tomatillo-Avocado Salsa, 116
    Ga Xao Xa Ot (Spicy Lemongrass Chicken), 118
    Honey Buffalo Pimento Mac n' Cheese, 123
    Santa Monica's Whole Roasted Chicken, 120

Prairie Grass Café, 73

Proxi, 44

Publican, The, 80

Publican's Veal Sweetbreads, The, 81

Purple Pig, The, 92

R

Ravioli Quattro Formaggi (Four Cheese Ravioli), 27

Rigatoni with Crispy Prosciutto and Vodka Sauce, 41

Risotto Certosino, 57

Roanoke, 12

Robert Et Fils, 133

Rose Mary, 107

S

Salmon Tartare with Doenjang and Yuzu Crème Fraîche, 65

Santa Monica's Whole Roasted Chicken, 120

Saranello's, 35

Scotch Eggs with Salad and Mustard Vinaigrette, 110

Shrimp Dejonghe, 69

Signature Room at the 95th, The, 68

Smoked Trout Salad, 19

Smyth and the Loyalist, 137

Spinach and Ricotta Gnocchi, 36

Salads
    Baby Beet and Farro Salad with Avocado, Tarragon, and Goat's Milk Feta, 12
    Harvest Salad with Quick-Pickled Summer Beans, 3
    Smoked Trout Salad, 19

Starters
    Brazilian Cheese Bites, 8
    Croquettes with Dijonnaise Dipping Sauce, 22
    Homemade Labneh (and Whey Brine), 6
    Muhammara, 17
    Okonomiyaki (Savory Japanese Pancake), 4
    Stuffed Colombian Arepas with Berkshire Pork Belly, Plantain, Black Beans, and Jicama, 11
    Stuffed Focaccia with Mozzarella, Taggiasca, Olives, and Basil, 15

Steamed Mussels with Lobster Butter Sauce, 61

Stuffed Colombian Arepas with Berkshire Pork Belly, Plantain, Black Beans, and Jicama, 11

Stuffed Focaccia with Mozzarella, Taggiasca, Olives, and Basil, 15

Summer House, 119

Superkhana International, 124

Swift & Sons, 96

T

Tacos Al Pastor (Spit-Roasted Pork Tacos), 95

Takito Kitchen, 10

Takito Street, 10

Tomato and Summer Squash Gratin, 38

Topolobampo, 114

Tree House, 40

U

Urban Belly, 98

V

Veal

Walnut Crusted Veal Rib Eye with Gratin of Cauliflower, Pink Peppercorns, Confit Garlic, and Sage, 76

Publican's Veal Sweetbreads, The, 81

Vie (Western Springs), 2

W

Walnut Crusted Veal Rib Eye with Gratin of Cauliflower, Pink Peppercorns, Confit Garlic, and Sage, 76

Wild Striped Bass with Sweet Corn Chowder and Littleneck Clams, 44

Wisconsin Trout Soup with Potato-Infused Cream and Bacon, 53

X

XOCO, 114

ABOUT THE AUTHOR

Amelia Levin is an award-winning, Chicago-based freelance writer, magazine editor, cookbook author, and certified chef who writes about food, food service, and the restaurant industry. She has authored several cookbooks, and her work has appeared in a variety of food industry B2B magazines, including the American Culinary Federation's bi-monthly magazine *National Culinary Review*, for which she currently serves as editor-in-chief. A die-hard Chicagoan, Amelia was born and raised in Chicagoland and has lived in the city for two decades, most recently moving back to her hometown of Highland Park with her husband Harvey, son Jonah, and daughter Lily. View her work at amelialevin.com.